THE
RIDGEWAY

THE RIDGEWAY

Neil Curtis

Photographs by Martin Trelawney
General editor Michael Allaby

AURUM PRESS

COUNTRYSIDE COMMISSION · ORDNANCE SURVEY

ACKNOWLEDGEMENTS

In no particular order, my thanks go to the series editor, Michael Allaby, for asking me to compile this guide; to Wendy Pettigrew of the Countryside Commission for her courteous co-operation; to David Venner, the Ridgeway Officer without whose help much of the information contained here could not have been pieced together; to Martin Trelawney for providing such splendid photographs with little help from me; to Ridgeway Warden Frank Hart, for sharing his knowledge of the sheep fairs at East Ilsley; to Ken Watts for his information on Snap; to my secretary, Trisha Walters, who despite the continued machine-gun noise of the wind on my dictating machine managed to type up my notes from which I then wrote this little book; and lastly, but by no means least, to my wife Sheila Dallas, who walked with me for the first 15 miles and who then provided logistical and moral support at various intervals along the way, as well as afterwards when I was struggling to put fingers to keyboard.

Neil Curtis has a degree in geology and has worked in natural history publishing since 1971. He lives in Oxfordshire and runs his own publishing service.

This edition first published 1989 by Aurum Press Ltd in association
with the Countryside Commission and the Ordnance Survey
Reprinted 1990
Text copyright © 1989 by Aurum Press Ltd, the Countryside
Commission and the Ordnance Survey
Maps Crown copyright © 1989 by the Ordnance Survey
Photographs copyright © 1989 by the Countryside Commission

British Library Cataloguing in Publication Data

Curtis, Neil.
The Ridgeway. – (National trail guides; 4)
1. Southern England. Long-distance footpaths: Ridgeway Path. Recreations:
Walking – Visitors' guides
I. Title II. Series
796.5'1'09422

ISBN 1 85410 019 X
OS ISBN 0 319 00170 9

Book design by Robert Updegraff
Cover photograph: view from Wainhill towards Bledlow
Title page photograph: the Chiltern escarpment from Watlington Hill

Typeset by Wyvern Typesetting Ltd, Bristol
Printed and bound in Italy by Printers Srl, Trento

CONTENTS

Circular walks appear on pages 32, 52, 58, 72, 78 and 118

How to use this guide

This guide to the 85-mile (137-kilometre) national trail along the Ridgeway is in three parts:

- The introduction, with an historical background to the area and advice for walkers and riders.

- The Ridgeway itself, split into twelve chapters, with maps opposite the description for each route section. In some cases the chapters cover relatively short sections of the Ridgeway, which will make it easier for people planning day or weekend walks or rides along this national trail. The distances noted with each chapter represent the total length of the Ridgeway, including sections through towns and villages. This part of the guide also includes information on places of interest as well as a number of short walks which can be taken around the Ridgeway. There are also many other circular routes linking with the Ridgeway, details of which are included in the relevant chapters. Key sites are numbered both in the text and on the maps to make it easier to follow the route description.

- The last part includes useful information such as local transport, accommodation and organisations involved with the Ridgeway.

The maps have been prepared by the Ordnance Survey for this trail guide using 1:25 000 Pathfinder maps as a base. The line of the Ridgeway is shown in yellow, with the status of each section of the trail – footpath, bridleway or byway, for example – shown in green underneath (see key on inside front cover). These rights of way markings also indicate the precise alignment of the Ridgeway. In some cases, the yellow line on these maps may show a route which is different from that shown on older maps; you are recommended to follow the yellow route in this guide, which will be the route that is waymarked with the distinctive acorn symbol 🟢 used for all national trails. Any parts of the Ridgeway that may be difficult to follow on the ground are clearly highlighted in the route description. *Black arrows (➡) at the edge of the maps indicate the start point.*

Should there be a need to divert the Ridgeway from the route shown in this guide, for maintenance work or because the route has had to be changed, you are advised to follow any waymarks or signs along the path.

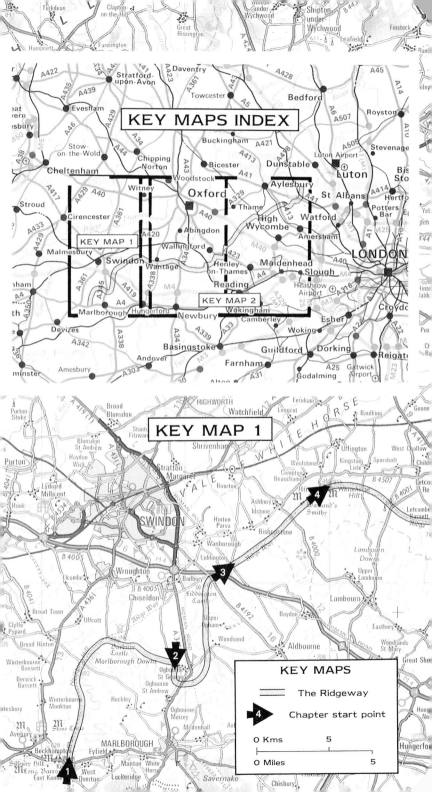

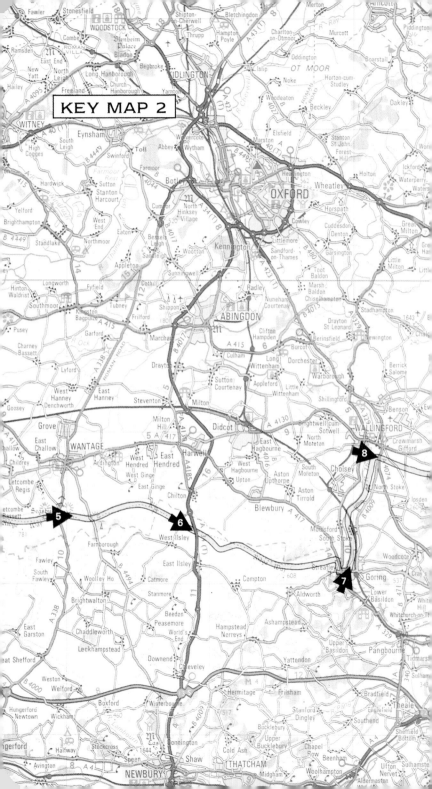

KEY MAP 2

Distance checklist

The following distances along the Ridgeway are included to help you plan your journey.

location	approx. distance from previous location	
	miles	*km*
Overton Hill	0	0
Barbury Castle (car park)	6.5	10.5
Ogbourne St George	2.6	4.2
Fox Hill	7.4	11.9
Ashbury (B 4000)	3.3	5.3
Uffington Castle/Whitehorse Hill	2.1	3.4
Sparsholt Firs	2.9	4.7
Manor Road (for Wantage)	3.4	5.5
Bury Down	5.7	9.2
Compton – bridleway access	2.9	4.7
Streatley (A 329)	5.2	8.4
Goring on Thames	0.4	0.6
South Stoke	1.8	2.9
North Stoke	2.3	3.7
Mongewell Park (for Wallingford)	1.2	1.9
Nuffield Common	4.0	6.4
Watlington (Hill Road)	5.4	8.7
Lewknor – road access	2.3	3.7
Chinnor	3.3	5.3
Princes Risborough (Brimmers Road)	5.3	8.5
Wendover	5.9	9.5
Wigginton	6.1	9.8
Tring Station	2.0	3.2
Ivinghoe Beacon	3.5	5.6

Preface

The Ridgeway is one of the national trails in England and Wales which the Countryside Commission promotes for walkers or riders to explore and enjoy the best of our countryside, far away from towns, traffic and the bustle of urban life.

These trails are particularly suited for long journeys, but they can also be sampled on an afternoon or over a weekend. Another way of using them is as part of a round trip, or circular walk, and suggestions for these are included in this guide. National trails are maintained by local authorities on behalf of the Commission, and are well waymarked with our distinctive acorn. Each trail provides an enjoyable, and sometimes challenging, walk or ride in the countryside.

National trails run through the grandest and most beautiful countryside and coast which England and Wales have to offer. Many of them also link with other waymarked paths, thus making it possible to plan a variety of journeys throughout the countryside.

We hope you will enjoy walking or riding along the Ridgeway and that this guide will help to make your journey one to remember.

Sir Derek Barber
Chairman
Countryside Commission

Thurle Down, near Streatley. Once the downs were predominantly grassland, but many have now been ploughed for arable crops.

PART ONE

INTRODUCTION

In *The Oldest Road: An Exploration of the Ridgeway*, J. R. L. Anderson states that 'Most roads have a beginning and an end, but the Ridgeway has neither: what is left of it, and it is a remarkable stretch for a road of such antiquity, starts nowhere and concludes in time rather than in space.' Historically and philosophically, this may be true but, for the purposes of this book and the Countryside Commission, the national trail begins in the west at Overton Hill, beside the A4 trunk road a short distance from the village of Avebury, a World Heritage site, with its extraordinary stone circles, and stretches eastwards for some 85 miles (137 km) ending at the triangulation pillar on Ivinghoe Beacon in Buckinghamshire, to the north-east of Tring. Thus, it is a convenient and satisfying route, starting and finishing as it does on hills, with parking, bus routes, and, in the case of Tring, railway stations nearby.

Passing through five counties (Wiltshire, Oxfordshire, Berkshire, Buckinghamshire and Hertfordshire) and crossing the chalk downland of the North Wessex Downs Area of Outstanding Natural Beauty (AONB), the Ridgeway goes through the Goring Gap, before following the River Thames for a short way and rising on to the undulating hills of the Chilterns AONB via Grim's Ditch. Thus the west–east walker gradually gathers an intimate experience of the landscape of this stretch of south-central England. For those who believe that the whole of this part of the country is nothing but motorways, industrial estates and urban conurbations, to walk the Ridgeway in its entirety is an education as well as a joy. That is not to say that, from time to time, the drone of speeding motor traffic does not intrude, nor that 'civilisation' is never encountered but, for much of the way, even in the mechanised, urbanised, computerised 20th century, it is possible to feel, if not 'far from the madding crowd', at least spiritually removed and moderately distanced from it. Indeed, one of the minor problems encountered by walkers tackling the whole route is that, especially along the western 'half', to find accommodation it is necessary to leave the ridge and descend as much as 3 miles (5 km) to a village, only to have to climb up again the next day.

We might like to believe that to walk the Ridgeway from Overton Hill to Streatley before crossing the Thames is to travel along an ancient trading route, remote from our world and unspoiled by human interference. Certainly the green road is an old one and, apart from the ever-spreading sprawl of Swindon (Swine Down), there are few towns or cities to bar the way. But, in some ways, it is along the less historically authentic part of the walk, from Goring to Ivinghoe, that more traditional kinds of landscape are encountered, even though the walker passes close to, or through, a number of small towns.

It is remarkable how quickly the mind adjusts, how scenery which had scarcely changed for decades, or even centuries, can be wiped away almost overnight, and yet how soon one forgets the former and accepts the latter as 'natural' rural England. Much of the western part of the Ridgeway follows a line of chalk downland where traces of ancient field systems show that prehistoric practice was markedly different in its use of land from our own and where the blackthorn-hedged, sheep- and rabbit-cropped fields still extant in this century have given way to vast, prairie-like expanses of monoculture grazing and monotonous hybrid cereal crops. In late summer, hectare upon hectare of uniformly golden, poker-straight, tall stems wave their abundance in the wind; on the grasslands even the sheep grow more quickly, more uniformly, and with leaner meat or less oily wool to satisfy the demands of today's consumers. But still, for those young enough to know nothing different or for walkers who are new to this trail, the Ridgeway seems to fulfil a basic need in many of us: a need to get away from city hurly-burly, to breathe fresh air, to view open, rolling land, to chance upon wild plants and animals, to encounter other occasional adventurers along the way, and to spend a few days at one's own pace.

Throughout its length, the Ridgeway is a versatile route. For anyone who is physically fit and who derives pleasure from testing their body and mental fortitude against distance, it is perfectly possible to complete the whole route in four days or even less, averaging more than 20 miles (32 km) a day. Unless walking the path is an exercise in stamina, to complete it at a more leisurely and enjoyable pace should take about six days, so that a day's walk is about 12–15 miles (20–25 km). A reasonable pace to maintain is about $2\frac{1}{2}$ miles (4 km) an hour, so 15 miles (25 km) might take a little over six hours. During three seasons of the year, this leaves you with plenty of time to stand and stare, to stop for feeding and watering, to chat with companion or passerby, and to investigate an ancient hill fort or a medieval church. Even in the winter, a day's walk of this distance should be perfectly possible if you are so inclined.

But there are other ways of travelling the Ridgeway. There are circular routes for walkers or riders, both official and unofficial, based on parts of its length and up to 8 miles (12 km) or so long. There are short strolls from a car park to a hill fort or a burial chamber such as Wayland's Smithy. It would be possible to take two cars and park one at each end of a day's stretch. You could tackle, as I have done more than once, Overton Hill to Streatley and Goring to Ivinghoe as two separate long weekend walks, or either could be shortened slightly to fit comfortably into a normal weekend.

Nor are you confined to Shanks's pony, for much of the western 'half' of the path is byway or 'road used as public path' (RUPP) and parts of the eastern section are bridleway. Horseriders and cyclists are permitted on bridleways (way-marked with blue arrows) and on byways (marked with red arrows). In addition, motorcycles and other motor vehicles are permitted on byways and most RUPPs. RUPPs are an old classification and all RUPPs are being reclassified as either byways or bridleways, but it will take some time to complete this work.

To some people, motorcycles and four-wheel-drive vehicles are sometimes rather too much in evidence on the western section of the Ridgeway, although it must be agreed that the current voluntary ban on summer Sundays and bank holidays does seem to have reduced the traffic or, at the very least, has tended to make the motorcyclists, especially, more sensitive to the likes and dislikes of other users. Finally, both children and adults, launching model gliders, powered craft, or even themselves attached to hang gliders, seem to find parts of the Ridgeway particularly suitable, as every walker discovers at the weekend or bank holiday in clement weather.

However you tackle the Ridgeway, it is there to be enjoyed and there is much to enjoy. From ridgetop to valley, from hill fort to chalk quarry, from trunk road to narrow track, a traveller on the Ridgeway will be accompanied by the rush of the wind, the songs of birds, the quiet rustle of wheat, and by the knowledge that he or she is following a path that has been trodden more or less continuously over much of its length for thousands of years.

History of the Ridgeway

The Ridgeway, of which the national trail forms a part, has been said to be one of the oldest 'roads' in Europe, although it seems that there is no direct evidence of its use before the Bronze Age. From the coast, perhaps near Lyme Regis in Dorset, the way stretched for more than 250 miles (400 km) in a north-easterly direction, probably reaching what is now the Wash somewhere near Hunstanton in north Norfolk. It is possible to walk this entire route today by first taking the Wessex Ridgeway (a Ramblers' Association-devised route) from Lyme Regis to Marlborough, and then the Ridgeway, and on to the Icknield Way to link with the Peddars Way, ending at Holme next the Sea.

The name 'Ridgeway' is taken from the Anglo-Saxon word 'hrycweg' and, in the various charters of their period, a complicated network of these green roads is mentioned – each usually following a natural route on high ground, thereby allowing the traveller to avoid the hazards of the densely wooded and often marshy ground of the valleys below, especially during the harsh weather of winter.

Most authorities agree, however, that the western half of the Ridgeway, in particular, must have been used as a drove road, a trading route, and as a convenient means for invaders, peaceful or war-like, to penetrate the heartland of southern England long before Anglo-Saxon or even Roman times, not least because of the numbers and scale of hill forts and ancient and important religious centres that grew up along its way, the remains of which we can still see today.

It is tempting to suppose that one is walking on identical ground to that trodden by the ancients. However, until about 200 years ago, the Ridgeway was a broad band of tracks along the crest of the Downs, or, in the case of the Icknield Way, beneath the scarp of the Chilterns. People walked, rode their horses or drove their sheep and cattle along the driest or most convenient track.

It was the Enclosure Acts of 1750–1800 that defined, for each parish, the course and exact width of the Ridgeway. For most parishes this was set at 40 feet (12 metres), for others at as much as 66 feet (20 metres). The banks and thorn hedges alongside the Ridgeway date from this period and were put there to prevent livestock from straying into the newly cultivated arable fields.

It is largely in this century that the present system of main, trunk and motorway roads has come into being, with some following the lines of older routes, such as Roman roads. And with the coming of the new means of communication, so the old ways have fallen into disuse except as convenient access roads for farmers or as footpaths and rights of way for today's nomads – walkers, horseriders and cyclists. Thus, in most places, only fragments of these ancient ways survive and we are fortunate that so much of the Ridgeway is now preserved.

The idea for a long-distance route following the line of the Chilterns and the Wessex chalk downs was first mooted in 1947 in a report by the Hobhouse Committee. The present route was approved by the Secretary of State for the Environment in 1972 and so began yet another phase in the long history of an ancient green road. Today, there is a Ridgeway Officer, based with Oxfordshire County Council's Department of Leisure and Arts, whose task it is to manage the national trail.

Practical advice

Walking, cycling or riding a horse on the Ridgeway does not require the same precautions as pursuing these activities on a mountain in Wales or Scotland. The weather is rarely very severe; it is hard to get lost; the going underfoot is not dangerous and is, at worst, wet and rutted; and you are seldom far from help should it be needed. On the other hand, there is no point in making life difficult for yourself and a few simple precautions should enhance your enjoyment.

If you are walking, the single most important piece of equipment to get right is footwear. Almost everyone who ever sets foot to footpath has a different view on what it is best to wear on the feet but one thing is certain, unless you usually live in them, you don't need foot-dragging heavy mountain boots here. For short walks, especially during winter or spring when parts of the way might be very boggy, wellington boots or one of the other kinds of rubber boots now available are as good as anything. But I would not advise wearing wellies for more than a day. For me the best compromise is a pair of modern lightweight walking boots or shoes.

Clothing, too, has come a long way since the mandatory tweeds and cords for the great outdoors but again it's up to you to find out what suits you best. For three seasons of the year, a pair of polycotton walking trousers, a shirt, a spare sweater or thermofleece garment, and a waterproof (preferably breathable)

Ogbourne St George, the only village to be found on the western section of the Ridgeway.

are all you really need. In winter, extra warm clothing, a hat and gloves are a good idea.

If I am out for the day or longer, I usually carry a small first-aid kit containing some aspirin, plasters, some 'moleskin', 'animal wool', or chiropodist's felt, a tube of antiseptic cream and, during the season, some antihistamine cream.

Especially on the western half of the walk, where pubs and cafés are well off the path, you will need to take some spare food and drink with you on a longer trip. For me it's usually a flask of coffee, an aluminium bottle of fresh water, a hunk of cheese, some wholemeal bread or rolls, something sweet, and something fruity. On the other hand, some people prefer to content themselves with a hearty breakfast and walk through until the end of the day and a substantial dinner.

This guide book, together with the waymarks you will find along the whole length of the path, will enable you easily to follow the route without any other assistance although, from time to time, signs do get vandalised and acorn symbols on trees need to be repainted. You do not necessarily require one, but it can be very satisfying to carry a compass with you and know how to use it. If nothing else, it might enable you more easily to identify features off the track.

To carry your bits and pieces, you will need a rucksack. Buy the best that you can afford. Try several sorts for comfort (especially with some weight in it) and access to its various pockets and compartments. It's very frustrating to have to undo lots of buckles, strings and zips and then empty the whole thing just to find your sandwiches at lunchtime. Remember, though, that even if you treat the seams with a sealing compound, rucksacks are rarely completely waterproof and it's a good idea to contain most of your belongings inside plastic bags within the rucksack. Don't be tempted to load up with the kitchen sink – a loaded rucksack will become very heavy after the first mile or two. Keep the weight down! Also, do remember that you should not leave any valuables in your car – take all cameras, money, etc. with you.

It is possible to find places to camp at intervals along most of the route although, unless you are on an official camp site where you will need to check in anyway, you must always seek permission to do so. There is a very wide variety of 'hi-tech' and 'not-so-hi-tech' lightweight tents to choose from. But, if you camp, you will need a bigger rucksack to cope with your tent and sleeping bag. Of course, it is perfectly possible to walk the whole route making use of youth hostels, guest houses, inns and hotels, thus avoiding the necessity to carry too much as you go along.

Horseriders and cyclists will find the going heavy after wet weather. Waterlogged ruts pose problems to the thoroughbred and the racing bike in almost equal measure! In a dry summer the ruts set rock hard and flints might occasionally puncture feet or tyres. But if these difficulties are avoided, the whole of the western half, and the Icknield Way section from west of Watlington to east of Chinnor, will provide pleasant and challenging conditions for two to three days' riding. If you wish to link these two sections, there is the Swan's Way Long Distance Bridleway, set up by Buckinghamshire County Council, which runs from Goring on Thames via the Icknield Way to Chinnor and then northwards to Salcey Forest in Northamptonshire. Details of accommodation on the Ridgeway sections – for both horse and rider – will be found on pages 137–9.

PART TWO

The Ridgeway

The 'grey wethers' – sarsen stones – on Overton Down. The boulders consist of cemented sandstone.

1 Overton Hill to Ogbourne St George

via Barbury Castle and Smeathe's Ridge
9 miles (14.7 km)

We begin our journey at the junction of the western end of the Ridgeway with the A4 trunk road at Overton Hill **1**, some $4\frac{1}{2}$ miles (7 km) west of the attractive Wiltshire town of Marlborough with its many shops, pubs and cafés. No visit to this part of England or any Ridgeway expedition would be complete, however, without exploring the village of Avebury **2** with its extraordinary stone circles and other features of interest (see page 34). Avebury is about $1\frac{1}{2}$ miles (2.5 km) to the north-west of our starting point and can be reached by driving for a little under three-quarters of a mile (1 km) along the A4 Devizes road and then turning right almost opposite West Kennett Farm on to the B4003, which takes you into the partially restored and so-called Stone Avenue leading to the Avebury monument.

The most convenient way of getting to Overton Hill is by car. If your intention is to walk the whole of the Ridgeway, then perhaps you can persuade someone to take you there or, if you are planning merely a day's or half day's walk (this section, for example) and you are walking with a companion, then it is a good idea to leave a car at each end of the section where there is suitable parking space. Even though there is adequate parking at Overton Hill, actually getting in and out of the parking area can be hazardous because of the busy A4 road at this point. When approaching from either direction, turning off the road must be undertaken near the brow of the hill and the view of the road from either side is limited, so it is vital to signal well in advance and to leave or rejoin the road as quickly as is safely possible. A useful landmark to the starting point is the Ridgeway Café, essentially a transport establishment, immediately to the west of the beginning of the path itself. It is an unattractive building but has a large car park at the front and, when it is open, it is possible to have a perfectly adequate meal there.

If you are planning to leave your car for any length of time, however, there is hard standing for quite a few cars on the entrance to the path itself.

Although it is less easy, and requires a bit more planning, it is perfectly possible to reach Overton Hill by public transport using the rail service to Swindon or Pewsey (see page 34 for route from Pewsey to Overton Hill) and/or buses from Swindon, Devizes and Marlborough to Avebury. From Avebury, it is then just a short road walk to the start of the route, or the Ridgeway can be picked up a little further along its way by following Green Street or the Herepath **3** (a name derived from the Old English word 'here', meaning army, and indicating that the path was wide enough for an army to move along it), which runs roughly north-east out of Avebury rings. This option avoids having to walk along any busy roads and can, therefore, be more pleasant than starting from Overton Hill. Also, if you are walking east to west, it provides a marvellous descent directly to Avebury, where the tea rooms (in summer) and the pub will be most welcome.

At Overton Hill **1** the Ridgeway is clearly indicated by a modern signpost and an older concrete Ridgeway marker. In this part of England, however, it is impossible to forget our ancient past for long, and a small collection of round barrows can be seen to the right of the beginning of the route. From Overton Hill, head almost due north and on to the Marlborough Downs – here known as Overton Down with Fyfield Down to the east.

As the route takes you uphill – steadily at first and then in more up-and-down fashion – the downlands to right and left are open and undulating. The fields are large, bounded mainly by fences of barbed or pig wire, and there are few trees. After a little over a mile (about 2 km) of comparatively easy walking along a wide track deeply rutted by farm vehicles, two groups of round barrows capped with trees come into view. Presumably, the trees remain because the mounds resist the plough although, despite evidence of some arable planting, this is mainly sheep- and cattle-grazing land. To the east of the track, the Ordnance Survey map suggests that there is evidence of Iron Age field systems and, although to the untrained eye they may not be obvious, some very low, quite straight banks bounding square or rectangular areas can be seen (or imagined?).

About 1½ miles (a little over 2 km) from Overton Hill, the Ridgeway route comes to a crossing of ways on Overton Down. To the south, from whence you have come, Overton Hill and the Bath Road are indicated and ahead, in a direction a little east of north, Hackpen Hill and Barbury Castle. To the west is Avebury, via the Herepath mentioned earlier, and to the east is Fyfield Down National Nature Reserve **4**. This has been described as one of the best preserved areas of ancient landscape in the vicinity. Throughout the 1960s, excavations

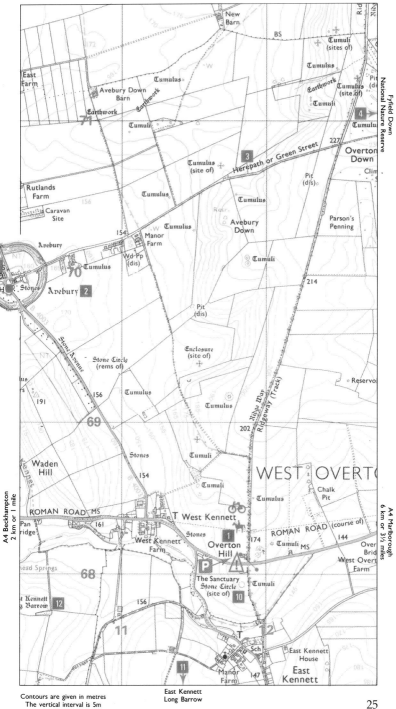

New Barn

BS

Tumuli (sites of)

Tumulus

Tumulus

East Farm

Avebury Down Barn

Earthwork

Earthwork

Earthwork

Tumulus

Cumuli (site of)

Tumuli

Tumulus

Herepath or Green Street

Overton Down

Tumulus (site of)

227

Tumulus

Rutlands Farm

Caravan Site

Tumulus

Tumulus

Pit (dis)

Parson's Penning

Manor Farm

Avebury Down

Avebury

Wd-Pp (dis)

Tumulus

Cumuli

214

Stones

Avebury

Pit (dis)

Stone Avenue

Enclosure (site of)

Reservoir

Stone Circle (rems of)

Tumulus

Ridge Way (Track)

Tumulus

202

Waden Hill

Stones

Tumuli

WEST OVERTON

Tumuli

Chalk Pit

ROMAN ROAD MS

West Kennett

Cumulus

Pan ridge

161

Stones

ROMAN ROAD (course of)

174

Tumuli

144

West Kennett Farm

Overton Hill

MS

West Overton Farm

head Springs

The Sanctuary Stone Circle (site of)

Tumuli

Kennett Barrow

156

East Kennett House

Sch

East Kennett

Manor Farm

147

East Kennett Long Barrow

A4 Beckhampton
2 km or 1 mile

Fyfield Down
National Nature Reserve

A4 Marlborough
6 km or 3½ miles

carried out here by the archaeologist Peter Fowler revealed evidence of agriculture, burial sites, settlements and of other features which might unravel the mysteries of what may have been a considerable civilisation.

Shortly after the crossing of these ancient tracks, you pass another footpath off to the right and aiming in a south-easterly direction. Hereabouts, to the left of the path, there is evidence of earthworks on the hill, while on the right the 'Pits (dis)', as shown on the Ordnance Survey map, are quite clearly visible. However, of the sarsen stones – the 'Grey Wethers', as they are sometimes called – I could see little from the Ridgeway, although they are to be found on Monkton Down and Fyfield Down (see page 39).

This length of Ridgeway between Fyfield and Monkton Down reveals some interesting contrasts in flora, as well as being one of the quieter stretches where bird song and the wind in the trees are the only sounds you will hear. From the chalky soils of Fyfield Down, supporting short downland grasses, vetches and orchids, the soil becomes slightly acid as a result of clay overlying the chalk. Here, profuse hedgerows close in, long grasses and nettles predominate on the verges, and the occasional gorse bush is seen.

A little beyond Monkton Down there are more disused pits on the left, and here the track takes a sharp right and left before continuing more or less northwards again. At this point there is a junction with another path, again to the south-east, sign-posted to Rockley and passing through Totterdown Wood. (Note: some of the rights of way shown on the map to the west of the Ridgeway here have altered.) The track climbs a little more, reaching a height of some 900 feet (270 metres) here, and continues its undulating way on high ground passing Berwick Bassett Down on the left, finally ascending again almost to the summit of Hackpen Hill with its trig point a little to the right of the Ridgeway.

A little before Hackpen Hill, the route turns slightly, taking on a north-easterly direction and then, once the hill has been passed, descends a little to the minor road between the village of Broad Hinton to the north-west and Marlborough to the south-east. There is room here to park a few cars and there is a good panoramic view across the plain where the villages of Broad Hinton and Winterbourne Bassett are clearly visible. Also from here, to the south-west, can be seen the smallish, roughly circular knob of Windmill Hill **5**, lying the other side of

Winterbourne Monkton. Windmill Hill is the site of another Neolithic monument, known as a causewayed enclosure, built about 3400 B C. It has been suggested that this 'camp' was a sort of New Stone Age social centre, and probably continued in use for almost 1,500 years.

From the road, the track, broad and rutted still, climbs a little and once again reaches a height of over 900 feet (270 metres) after another half mile (1 km) or so of walking. To the right is Preshute Down.

From here, the way begins to descend, bears a little more easterly, and then the impressive ramparts of Barbury Castle **6**

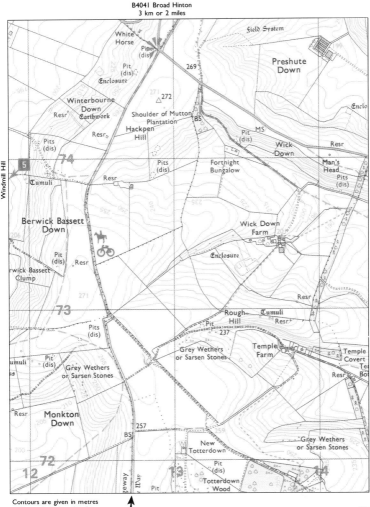

Contours are given in metres
The vertical interval is 5m

rear up ahead and to the right. As you reach the foot of Barbury Castle you meet a partially metalled road leading eventually to Wroughton in the north. Here the ancient Ridgeway, as marked on the Ordnance Survey map and according to other sources, branches left and heads north-east to the left of the lower slopes of the castle towards Chiseldon, which is some 4 miles (6 km) away.

The Ridgeway national trail, however, avoids the uninspiring village of Chiseldon, as well as some rather boring road walking, by taking you up the steep slopes to the top of the castle, across its interior, and then heads roughly south-eastwards past the information centre and car park, across another narrow metalled road towards Smeathe's Ridge.

The name Barbury is probably derived from the Anglo-Saxon 'Beran Byrg', which means 'Bera's Hill' after the Saxon chief, Bera, whose victory in A D 565 over the indigenous Romano-British forces effectively brought the latter's resistance to invasion to an end. This victory heralded the real beginning of the Anglo-Saxon period even though Saxon mercenaries had been brought to Britain by the Romans as early as the turn of the 5th century, and Saxon forces had been pushing steadily westwards from about A D 440 until A D 500.

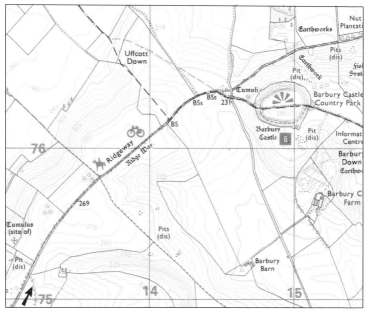

Contours are given in metres
The vertical interval is 5m

The ramparts of Barbury Castle, a hill fort used from Iron Age to Saxon times.

Today, the lush turf and imposing ramparts of Barbury Castle provide an ideal spot to sit and muse on these historical events and, in fact, the area was established as a country park in 1972. To the east of the hill fort is a car park with a stone-built plinth carrying a steel plaque erected jointly by the Automobile Association and Wiltshire County Council to commemorate the official opening of the park. There is ample parking here **7**, toilets and information panels. (See page 56 for information about hill forts.) From the car park, you emerge along a rough track to reach the narrow, metalled road which approaches the car park entrance from the north. Turn right and it quickly deteriorates into a rough track, once again running south-eastwards, and passing Upper Herdswick Farm on the left. Shortly after you have passed the farm, there is a signposted turning off the track to the left through farm and pedestrian gates. Go through the gate, and continue along another farm track towards Smeathe's Ridge **8**.

Smeathe's Ridge is a prominent north-west to south-east feature in the landscape here, continuing for at least 1½ miles (2.5 km) towards Coombe Down to the west of Ogbourne St George. This is another ancient route, thought to have been used when the lower 'Old Ridgeway' across the plain was too wet. On either side of the chalk ridge the rounded hill slopes away quite sharply from its maximum elevation of over 700 feet (220 metres) so that the views to north and south are panoramic and there is a sense of space and airiness as you wander along the broad, grassy, gently undulating track. The scenery all around is now open, rolling farmland, with few fences or hedges. To right and left there is the occasional clump of trees and there are more scattered trees on Burderop Down to the north.

As I walked along one early spring morning, I was accompanied by the irregular shot-gun reports of automatic bird scarers which punctuated the more pleasing refrain of skylarks spiralling upwards in their songflight. After crossing a gate with a stile the going is simply a fairly well-defined path across grassland. The track continues to bear to the south-east with the high ground of Ogbourne Down and Coombe Down to the south and south-east respectively. There is some scattered evidence of the existence of tumuli here. Pass through another gate marked with the now familiar acorn symbol and a blue waymark arrow; at this point, on the hill to the right, look for the signs of erosion and soil creep. Now climb over another stile. From here, the track crosses a series of mounds and passes an

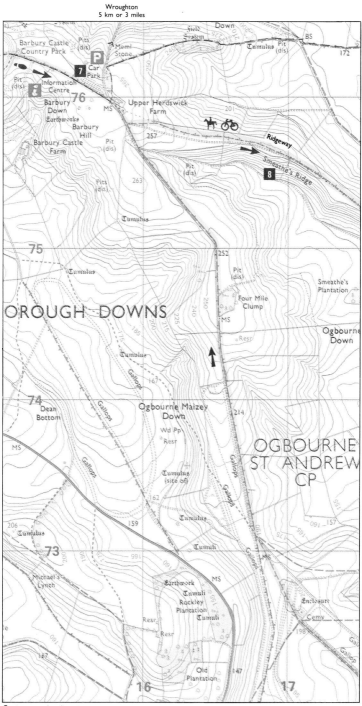

Wroughton
5 km or 3 miles

Down

Field System

Barbury Castle
Country Park

Pits (dis)

Memi Stone

Tumulus

Pit (dis)

BS

172

P

Car Park

7

Pit (dis)

Information Centre

i

76

Barbury Down

Earthworks

Barbury Hill

Barbury Castle Farm

Pit (dis)

MS

Upper Herdswick Farm

201

257

Ridgeway

263

Pit (dis)

Smeathe's Ridge

8

Pits (dis)

Tumulus

75

252

Pit (dis)

Smeathe's Plantation

Tumulus

Four Mile Clump

OROUGH DOWNS

225 240

MS

Resr

Ogbourne Down

Tumulus

Gallops

167

74

Dean Bottom

Ogbourne Maizey Down

214

MS

Gallops

Wd Pp

Resr

OGBOURNE ST ANDREW CP

Gallops

Tumulus (site of)

162

Gallops

Tumulus

159

206

Tumulus

73

Tumuli

Michael's Lynch

Earthwork

MS

Tumuli

Rockley Plantation

Tumuli

Enclosure

Cemy

Resr

Resr

187

Old Plantation

147

16

17

Contours are given in metres
The vertical interval is 5m

31

ugly concrete building with a steel door. Now you descend more or less eastwards towards the narrow, north–south road which takes a slightly offbeat route between Chiseldon to the north and Ogbourne St George. As you gradually lose height you cross another stiled gate, at which point the path becomes a more obvious farm track with tall hawthorn hedges on the right.

Arriving at the road, turn right – the direction is quite clearly indicated by the green metal 'Ridgeway' and acorn signpost. After about 100 yards (90 metres) the road turns sharply left and leads into the village of Ogbourne St George 9 itself. You can choose to detour through the village for refreshment or accommodation, or carry on along the Ridgeway which is signposted on the track to the right.

As you walk down the road to the village the red-brick, Georgian-style manor house comes into view on the left and close by is a grey, stone-built church. On the right is the attractive Tudor-style cottage known as The Kens. As you approach the pubs and the main A 345 road, the quaint village gives way to less appealing buildings and fast cars. There is a frequent, weekday Swindon to Marlborough bus service.

A CIRCULAR WALK FROM BARBURY CASTLE

$7\frac{3}{4}$ miles (12.5 km) *(see maps on pages 28–33)*

From Barbury Castle 6 and the car park 7, follow the Ridgeway route eastwards, as described in the main text, along Smeathe's Ridge to the road just before Ogbourne St George 9. Again turn right and follow the Ridgeway route but, after about half a mile (1 km), instead of turning left to Southend, continue straight on a little to the west of south to Ogbourne St Andrew. Follow the footpath past the church and on to Ogbourne Maizey where the path joins the road. Turn right and continue more or less westwards on the right of way which leaves the hamlet. The way turns to the north-west and then north, with gallops to the right for much of the way. (If the gallops are in use, short diversions may be indicated.) Continue back to Barbury Castle, along what was once an old coaching route between Swindon and Marlborough.

Further details of this walk can be found in *Circular Walks from The Ridgeway: Barbury Castle/Burderop Down/Smeathe's Ridge/The Ogbournes*, a leaflet published by Wiltshire County Council and included in the *Ridgeway Information Pack* (see page 141).

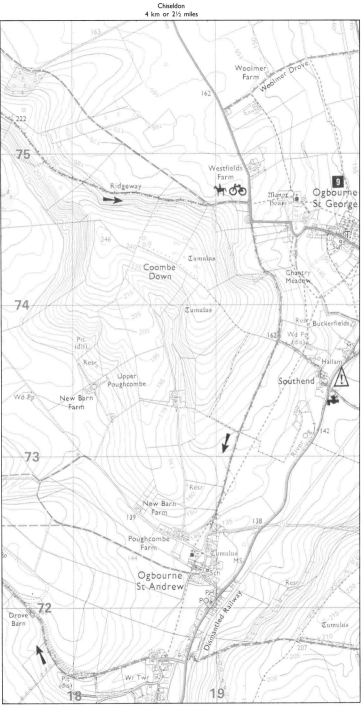

An alternative beginning: Pewsey to Overton Hill

An optional start (or end) to your Ridgeway journey is from Pewsey station, some 6 miles (10 km) from Overton Hill. It is a splendid excursion with some attractive scenery *en route*.

As you come out of Pewsey station, turn left and walk along the road to Pewsey Wharf, where there is a car park and toilets. Then take the Kennet and Avon Canal towpath in a westerly direction until you reach the second road bridge, at Wilcot. Turn right on to the main road towards Alton Priors. Almost immediately after the second turning to the right, signposted to Stowell and Oare, the road makes a sharp, left-hand bend. At this point, there is a green lane on the right (Workway Drove), and you should leave the road and join it. Continue uphill past Pewsey Downs National Nature Reserve until you reach the road. Cross into the field opposite and then bear right and follow the fence which leads uphill to Wansdyke. From Wansdyke, take the second path on the left through the woodland and keep straight on to East Kennett. In the village, take the road to the right, signposted to West Overton. After about 100 yards, go straight into a lane, keeping the stone wall on your left-hand side. Cross a bridge, walk up the left-hand edge of a field past the Sanctuary, and you will reach the starting point of the Ridgeway at Overton Hill.

The Avebury area

It is not uncommon that prehistoric, or even more recent historical, remains are less awe-inspiring on the ground than they appear on the map or from scientific descriptions proclaiming their archaeological significance. A good example of this is the so-called Sanctuary **10**, where all you can see is a pattern of concrete posts marking the points where stones and posts are said once to have stood. For all the casual observer can believe, the posts may be some kind of scientific practical joke! Not so with Silbury Hill, West Kennett Long Barrow **12**, Stonehenge, or especially the Avebury Stone Circles **2**. Indeed, in the latter case, the extraordinary nature of the megalithic construction almost beggars description. In the 18th century, though, even this prehistoric temple was not respected by local builders of a different age. They discovered that the stone from which the monument was constructed was good for more modern building work, and thus the temple, which had taken so much human effort to erect, was reduced to shattered remains.

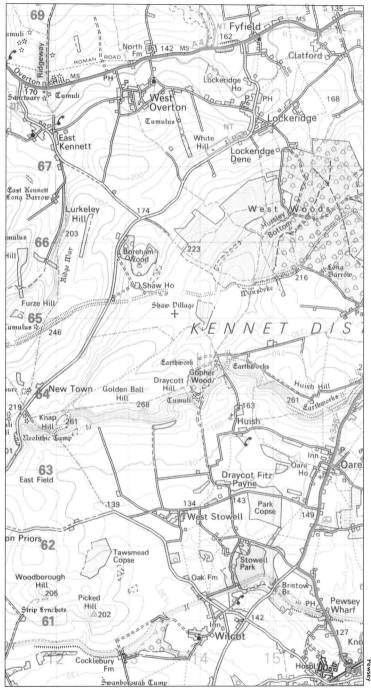

Contours are given in metres
The vertical interval is 10m

Scale is approx 1¼ inches to 1 mile

The Great Barn at Avebury housing the Wiltshire Folk Life Museum.

Avebury

A visit to the Alexander Keiller Museum at Avebury, opened originally in 1938, will, through its displays and literature, reveal a great deal about the cultures which held this spot in such high religious regard. Alexander was a Keiller of marmalade fame, and he lived in Avebury Manor from 1936 until he died in 1955. The land he acquired, and on which he began his excavations in 1934, was obtained by the National Trust in 1942 through a public appeal for funds. Avebury Stone Circle **2** is the largest monument of its kind in Britain, and possibly in the world. It dates from the late Neolithic period and was, therefore, constructed some 4,000 years ago. It consists of a roughly circular bank, which is now up to about 17 feet (5 metres) high but which must once have been of much greater proportion, enclosing an area of over 27 acres (11 hectares). The

bank is cut by a ditch and originally, on the inner edge of the ditch, there stood almost 100 of the great, undressed, natural sarsens, each of which may have weighed as much as 50 tons. The enclosure is effectively cut into four quadrants by entrances and there are two more circles, the northern Cove and the Southern Inner Circle, within the main enclosure.

It is generally thought that the Avebury Stone Circle represented a social and/or religious centre for the primitive farming communities which had become established on the Wessex downland because of the open, well-drained nature of the land. Such land lent itself to the farming methods practised by the people who had moved into the area from the European continent, probably via the Ridgeway.

Kennet District Council has published two useful leaflets: *Avebury: Archaeology of the District* and *A Day in Avebury*. Both are available from the Avebury tourist information centre.

The Sanctuary

At Overton Hill, opposite the start of the Ridgeway, is the Sanctuary **10**, referred to briefly earlier, which authorities now consider would be more properly named Overton Hill Circles because of the four distinct phases of construction which seem to have taken place here.

The Sanctuary was the name given in 1720 by William Stukely to two stone circles which stood at this point until 1724 when they were broken up. The antiquary, John Aubrey, also referred to this monument in 1648. The exact site of the stone circles was then lost, but it was recovered and excavated by M. E. and B. H. Cunnington in 1930. Rectangular concrete pillars have been used to mark the positions where stone holes have been found, while the six concentric rings of holes and the small central hole which once held wooden posts have been marked by round pillars. It has been suggested that the timber structures were replaced by the stone ones in the early Bronze Age when the West Kennett Avenue, linking Avebury with the Sanctuary, was also built.

It seems likely that the Sanctuary was erected for religious purposes and that the first quite small, rather flimsy hut was built on the site before 2500 BC during late Neolithic times, and that the rings of post holes represent successive phases of larger and more robust buildings perhaps completed more than 500 years later.

Long barrows

If you look almost due south from the Sanctuary, a long, tree-covered mound marks the site of another prehistoric site, East Kennett Long Barrow **11**. There is no public right of way to this site and the side ditches which once flanked the mound have now been ploughed over. No record exists to indicate that the barrow has been excavated, but it is almost certain that it is of the chambered type and similar to that of West Kennett Long Barrow **12** to the north-west of its eastern companion. These long barrows were chambered burial tombs which were in use for perhaps 1,000 years during late Neolithic times. In the case of the West Kennett Barrow, remains of at least 46 individuals who had been buried there have been uncovered during excavations of the site. The West Kennett site is well worth a visit now that it has been restored by the Department of the Environment, and access is via a track which leads from the A 4 about 1 mile (1.5 km) to the east of Beckhampton roundabout.

Sarsen stones

The word 'sarsen' is thought to have been derived from 'Saracen', and therefore sarsen or Saracen stones were believed to have been pagan monuments. In fact, these sometimes very large boulders of cemented sandstone which litter Fyfield Down are all that remains, after weathering and erosion, of a once continuous horizon of Tertiary sandstone that was deposited on the chalk.

A sidetrip into Fyfield Down National Nature Reserve is worthwhile. The Nature Conservancy Council has an information board by the Ridgeway where it is joined by the Herepath from Avebury; there are a number of paths through the Nature Reserve.

A sarsen on the Avenue at Avebury.

2 Ogbourne St George to Fox Hill

past Snap and Liddington Castle
7½ miles (11.9 km)

From Ogbourne St George **9** you can choose to rejoin the Ridgeway by the A 345 at Southend or return to the point where you left the route of the Ridgeway to turn left into the village. There you continue straight on, as indicated by the Ridgeway signpost, and dive into a tree-lined and partly sunken lane which can be quite muddy following wet weather. As it continues, a little to the east of south, the going remains rather muddy underfoot. It then ascends and, as it does, the lane becomes less sunken so that the village of Ogbourne St George can be seen to the left across the valley. After a little over 800 yards (730 metres) the Ridgeway takes a sharp turn to the left, and descends gently towards the road at the hamlet of Southend, the track becoming partially gravelled as you approach the houses, and then metalled. To the right of the road, an attractive collection of buildings comes into view. Some of these are part timbered and thatched, and look, at first sight, to be authentically Tudor. The road crosses a small bridge over the River Og, continues straight ahead, and crosses the busy A 345 road. Once over the road, you will find that the owner of the cottage facing the Ridgeway about 50 yards along on your right has provided a water tap on his front wall for thirsty travellers.

Once again, the track becomes a grassy sunken lane and gently climbs the hill. In about 440 yards it passes between the brick abutments of a former bridge which once carried a railway line from Chiseldon over the path, and here the route takes a more easterly turn. From this point, the incline gradually steepens as you approach a ridge and the route begins to head in a more north-easterly direction. By a newish house, the way crosses the Roman road which, as usual, runs arrow-straight and which, a little further north, provides the line for part of the A 345 road from Chiseldon.

To the left of the track a little further along, there is a wind pump and reservoir alongside some chalk pits. As the path continues to climb on to the ridge, the trees which obscured the scenery thin out and there are panoramic views to the north and west. A few hundred yards past the wind pump the slope gradually begins to ease as you approach the brow of the ridge.

To the right, on the map, the names Yielding Copse, the intriguing Oak Stagger and other 'copses' identify the various small woods in the area.

At a second crossing of the ways, the Ridgeway turns sharply to the left (north) at a corner where there is the site of another reservoir. Your route is clearly marked, however, and by now you have reached the height of 780 feet (237 metres), providing more panoramic views.

The way is broader now, and quite level, but has been surfaced with chalk which, in wet weather, can be very sticky. There are slight undulations along the muddy lane but the views, to the golf course and beyond, are still pleasant.

Approaching Chase Wood and Round Hill Downs, there is a rather ancient and rusting water tower which might perhaps have stored water from an underground spring to give a head of pressure for the buildings nearby. Turn left here on to the metalled farm road. This soon crosses the Aldbourne– Ogbourne St George road (called 'Copse Drove') and then you are on a green lane once again. In the flat fields to the right of the

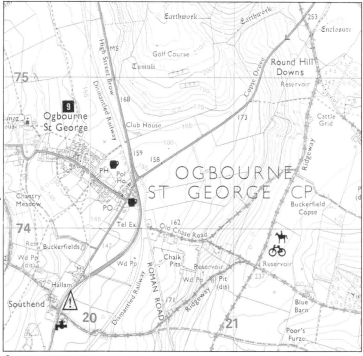

Contours are given in metres
The vertical interval is 5m

way, cereal crops may show green in April and, among them, the ground is thick with flinty shards and nodules. Flints protrude from the track, too, as I discovered once when I tripped over one! The going is also deeply rutted and muddy hereabouts.

This tree- and bush-lined green lane continues northwards for some 3 miles (5 km). About half a mile (1 km) beyond the metalled road, however, there is a crossing of the ways where the map marks a trig point, but a wooden signpost tells you to continue northwards. The track to the left, towards a mast, is clearly broad enough to carry vehicular traffic, but it is marked 'Public Footpath Only'. To the right the track leads to the abandoned village of Snap **13** (see page 47). There are also signs of a small underground reservoir here. On these dry, chalk ridges of the Wessex Downs, water has always been in short supply – perhaps the ancients made use of dew ponds? (See page 45.) Ahead, between the descent and the ascent to the slopes of Liddington Castle Fort **14**, there are fine views to the east and west.

Near the beginning of the slopes which eventually lead up to the hill fort, a gate temporarily bars the way. And here, to the right of the track, there is a clearly defined linear earthwork as you approach the fort which lies to the left and commands the heights of Liddington Hill: 911 feet (277 metres) at its summit, the highest point along the Ridgeway. As the ascent eases, the actual castle ramparts project slightly above the top of the hill. It must once have been a peaceful place, and it is still lovely with a sense of real height and isolation, but the noise from the M4 motorway tends to disturb the quiet. (A permissive path (not shown on the map) leads to the fort.)

Liddington Castle is also marked by a trig point, and a short diversion from the Ridgeway across the fields, thick with monoculture grass, brings you to the fort's ramparts. It should be noted that there is a permissive path leading around the edge of the field to Liddington, and the ramparts have been partly fenced off.

From the castle, the growing conurbation of Swindon can be seen to the north. The castle provides a good view of the lowlands all around and it is not hard to imagine why it was chosen as the site for a defensive earthwork. On the trig point is a plaque celebrating the fact that Liddington Hill was beloved by nationally known local authors, Richard Jefferies and Alfred Williams.

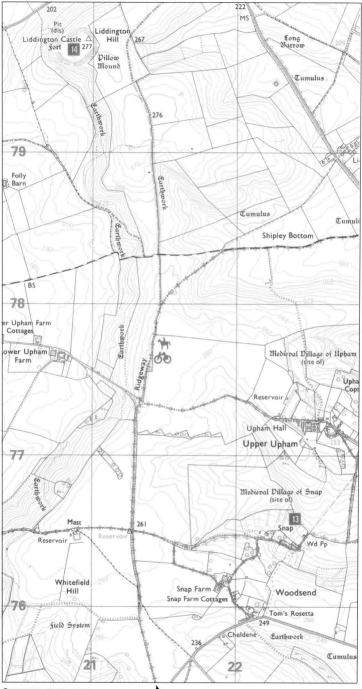

Contours are given in metres
The vertical interval is 5m

43

Leaving Liddington Hill, the Ridgeway veers from north to north-east. The track now descends towards the B4192 and the M4, and from the point at which the path meets the B4192 it follows roads for about 1¼ miles (2 km). When you reach the B4192, turn left on to it. (Note that there is also a path to the right which, in about 3½ miles (6 km) reaches the village of Aldbourne.) In a short distance, take the road to the right signposted to Little Hinton and Bourton. Soon after the turning to Manor Farm, the road passes over the M4 motorway – a chance, after more leisurely journeying, to reflect upon the pros and cons of motorised transport. The landmark to aim for is the radio mast at the top of Fox Hill, although you do not, in fact, arrive precisely at its foot. As you walk along the road, you will pass by the obliquely situated Front Lodge Cottages which stand guard to the entrance drive of King Edward's Place and, shortly afterwards, you cross yet another Roman road which has been adopted by modern route planners, the Ermin Way. And here, most welcome at the appropriate time of day, is the Shepherd's Rest public house **15** – one of the very few pubs you will pass which is actually on the route. There is car parking space further along at Fox Hill, and the village of Wanborough is just 1½ miles (2.5 km) away along the Ermin Way.

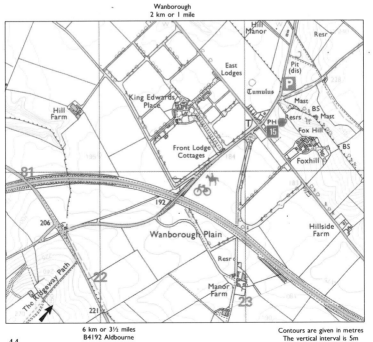

Wanborough
2 km or 1 mile

6 km or 3½ miles
B4192 Aldbourne

Contours are given in metres
The vertical interval is 5m

The origins of chalk

Most of the higher ground along which the Ridgeway makes its way consists of what is often described as Wessex chalk downland and the chalk hills of the Chilterns; for some reason, the latter countryside is referred to as downland only in some patches. Other national trails, such as the South Downs Way, also follow the line of a chalk scarp. A glance at a simple geological map shows that much of south-eastern England is situated on chalk rock which runs, like a three-pronged fork with a short handle, from the Dorset coast to north Norfolk with the two southern tines separated by the Weald and meeting the sea via the North and South Downs. It is these well-drained chalk uplands that have been used as areas on which to farm and on which lines of communication could be established away from the forested, marshy and hostile lands in the valleys below.

Many people, if asked to describe chalk, might well name the white sticks once used so commonly to write on school blackboards. In fact, chemically, this is a different material from that which is the foundation of Ridgeway country. On the other hand, most people have quite a good idea of typical chalk scenery with its rolling hills, springy, close-cropped turf, beech woodlands or wide-open arable land. But what is the chalk on which the land has evolved?

It has long been known that, chemically, chalk is largely calcium carbonate, that is lime, so it will effervesce in contact with an acid such as hydrochloric. Sometimes chalk may be stained reddish brown or yellowish orange with iron, and sometimes it is punctuated with layers of oddly shaped siliceous flints, but essentially chalk is white in colour so that if the turf is removed to form, say, a giant horse shape on a hillside, the figure can be seen standing out white against green for miles around. Chalk is permeable to water and, when soaked, it can be soft and sticky; if it is dry it seems as hard as any other stone. Its permeability to water allows the soils which form on it, shallow though they may be, to drain well. In fact, one of the problems of life on chalk country is the lack of permanent sources of water. It is this feature which led local people to excavate the so-called dew ponds.

The 19th century journalist and Wiltshire countryman, Richard Jefferies, described the way in which local people constructed dew ponds in his day by digging out a shallow pit

Chalk downland dominates the landscape of the western half of the Ridgeway.

over quite a large area. It would then be lined with impermeable clay, which had been mixed with soot to deter insects and worms from boring through it. As mist and low cloud condensed and any falling rain was captured, the pond would gradually fill with water. With natural waterways and springs in short supply high on the downs, these ponds were essential for stock in the days before a piped water supply was available.

In complete contrast to the general dryness of the chalk ridge, parts of the Ridgeway lie on fairly thick clay which overlies the chalk, especially on the hill tops. Examples are to be found in the Winterbourne Monkton Down/Hackpen Hill area, around the Wiltshire/Oxfordshire border near Bishopstone, and at Gramps Hill near Wantage. The clay-with-flints capping on the Chiltern escarpment causes similar conditions, giving rise to deep ruts or hoof-prints which fill with water in winter and often remain wet through much of the summer.

It has also long been known that chalk must have formed as a sediment in the sea but it was once thought to have been deposited in deep oceans because, in some ways, it resembles certain oozes which form in such places. It is now understood, however, that the great thicknesses of chalk which underlie the landscape were laid down in warm, shallow, clear seas that spread across much of what is now northern Europe more than 65 million years ago. It was deposited as a very fine-grained, calcareous mud, made up largely of countless billions of tiny shells, shell fragments and the remains of some small plants called coccolithophorids. The tiny, calcareous shells are known as coccoliths. The flints which are so often found in the upper layers of chalk are made up of silica but their exact origin remains uncertain. It may be that the compound which comprises them has resulted from a kind of 'gel' made from the solution of fragments of the skeletons of sea sponges.

Snap Village

In contrast to the ancient monuments seen so far along the Ridgeway, the site of the old village of Snap **13** is a more poignant reminder of changes in rural life. Snap was a very old settlement, dating back at least to 1377 when it was mentioned in connection with the Poll Tax, but by the turn of this century there were only a dozen cottages and a farm in the village. Changes in farming practices in the area, from labour-intensive arable farming to stock grazing that requires fewer workers, had meant that the residents of Snap eventually had to move elsewhere to find jobs.

By 1905 Snap was abandoned, although the farm itself lingered on to the 1930s. Now the outlines of the village can be seen best in the winter, although sarsen rubble marks the remains of the cottages. Sites abandoned in the 20th century are rare, and Snap is unique in Wiltshire; its story is outlined in a monograph to be published by the Wiltshire Library and Museum Service.

Certainly it is a good place to ponder about the current changes in rural life – will settlements be similarly deserted in the future, or will they survive? Compare Snap's fate with that of the villages of Lockinge and Ardington (see page 74) further along the Ridgeway – both have lessons for the future.

3 Fox Hill to Whitehorse Hill

past Ashbury and Uffington Castle
5½ miles (8.7 km)

From the crossroads and the Shepherd's Rest **15**, continue on the road, gently uphill and bearing slightly left, until after about 200 yards (180 metres) the Ridgeway bears right and north-east becoming a broad, chalky track as it does so. There is ample car parking here. The track is deeply rutted and can be very sticky in winter. In fact, this is the worst section of the Ridgeway, but after the Ashbury Road the going gets better. Good footwear is essential here!

After about 275 yards another track crosses the trail. On either side, the fields are open, arable land, and the map suggests that there are more reservoirs. From the path, looking to the north, the reservoir in front of the 832-foot (253-metre) summit and trig point of Charlbury Hill are apparent. To the right (south) is the open, rounded high ground of Lammy Down where, once again, there is a reservoir. There are ancient field systems and strip lynchets marked on the map on the Bishopstone side of the hills to the north, but these are not visible from the path. A lynchet or 'linch' is the line of a ridge marking the boundary of a prehistoric field, and was caused by soil slipping downhill as a result of ploughing, forming a ridge along the lower boundary of the field.

The Ridgeway first descends and then rises gently towards Ridgeway Farm, where a minor road from the village of Bishopstone **16**, about a mile (1.5 km) to the north, crosses the route. Part of the way down the hill towards Ridgeway Farm, a dog-leg farm track crosses the Ridgeway but you continue on the main path where, at the foot of the descent, another major right of way crosses the route which, in a northerly direction, also leads to Bishopstone; this track passes to the left (as we look at it) of a deep cut in the land.

Look from the path towards Charlbury Hill, mentioned earlier, in a direction which would now be just about due west, for traces of those ancient field systems. To the south and east, the countryside is open, gently rolling, with isolated lines and clumps of trees here and there, while to the north and west the land falls away more steeply to the flatter country around Bishopstone.

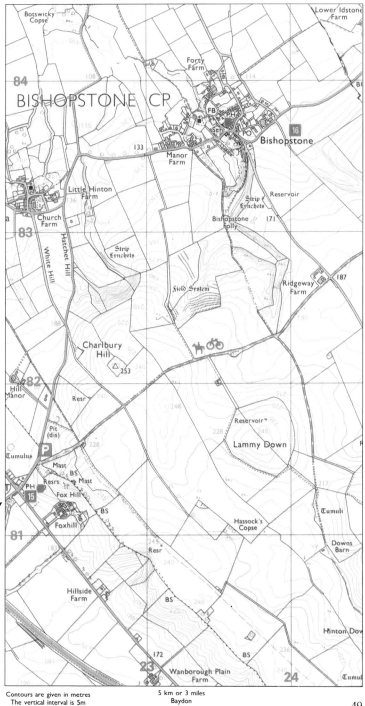

Botswicky Copse

Lower Idstone Farm

84

BISHOPSTONE CP

Forty Farm

FB
PH
Sch
PO

16

Bishopstone

133

Manor Farm

Reservoir

Strip Lynchets

Little Hinton Farm

83

Church Farm

Hatcher Hill

White Hill

Bishopstone Folly

171

Strip Lynchets

Field System

187

Ridgeway Farm

Charlbury Hill

253

82

Hill Manor

Resr

Reservoir

Lammy Down

Pit (dis)

Tumulus

P

Mast
BS
Resrs
Mast

PH
15
Fox Hill

BS

Foxhill

Hassock's Copse

Tumuli

81

Resr

Downs Barn

Hillside Farm

BS

172

Hinton Dow

23

Wanborough Plain Farm

BS

24

Tumul

Contours are given in metres
The vertical interval is 5m

5 km or 3 miles
Baydon

49

Clearly signposted, the way takes you straight on and, although the ruts persist, at least the walking is comparatively level. After less than 400 yards of easy going, the broad track begins to rise gently and, on both sides, the countryside is prairie-like, although there are some lines of trees to the south and west to break the monotony. About half a mile (1 km) beyond the road and Ridgeway Farm, you step out of Wiltshire and into Oxfordshire, the boundary being marked by a wooden post. From here to Idstone Hill, the map tells you that you have climbed a mere 66 feet (20 metres) but, on the ground, the ascent seems to be greater. Where the partly metalled and partly chalk-surfaced road crosses, continue to the north-east. There are farm buildings at the crossing, and drinking water can be had from a pathside tap. The way now levels out once again but soon becomes a deeply rutted tree-lined track.

Looking to right and left, as the path winds up between the trees, I found myself in April reflecting sadly on the prairie-style, monoculture farming. Perhaps as little as twenty years ago, the path would probably have been bounded by early spring flowers, but these have now given way to crops and pesticides in the interests of economy and efficiency and to provide consumers with cheap produce. In places here the ruts, made mainly by farm vehicles, I must surmise, are as much as 18 inches (45 cm) deep. This deep layer of clay masks the effects of the chalk which elsewhere lies near the surface and gives rise to a profusion of calcicolous plants. Here the paucity of flowers and associated animal life produced a rather dull and strangely quiet atmosphere, although oilseed rape, which takes the place of cereals these days, was just beginning to flower. And by the side of the path, from time to time, could be seen the tiny blue flowers of that charming little plant, the speedwell.

About an hour after leaving Fox Hill some 3 miles (5 km) behind, you arrive at the crossing of the B4000 road to Ashbury **17** where Ashbury Folly is marked on the map. However, if you are coming from the west and thinking of going into Ashbury, you may prefer to use the footpath which goes off to the left at the previous field boundary about half a mile before the road junction, rather than the 'B' road. All there is to see now is a little copse of trees. Ashbury, once officially praised as the best-kept village in England, is a little over half a mile (1 km) downhill along the road to the north-west. Anyone completing the western half of the Ridgeway in two days, as I have done, will find this a convenient stopping place. The path crosses the

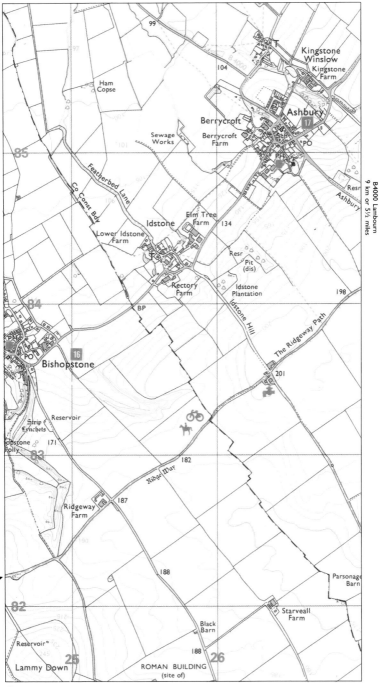

Contours are given in metres
The vertical interval is 5m

51

B4000 marching steadily north-eastwards, this time signposted to the ancient monument of Wayland's Smithy.

A little over 400 yards further on, a grassy farm track leads off to the left; the corner is marked on the map as Kingstone Barn but there is little trace here now of a barn except for the area of grass. And in another 400 yards there is a line of trees astride the Ridgeway. You are now beginning to climb again and then the way continues to be fringed with still more trees. After another 300 yards a track leads to Odstone Barn which, this time, is still standing. About 300 yards beyond this point, you come upon the path off to the left to Wayland's Smithy Long Barrow **18**, partly hidden among the trees. It is well worth a look and, on a rather bleak and wintry day, it feels a lonely place and few people would fail to be carried back in time (see page 57).

A CIRCULAR WALK TO ASHDOWN HOUSE AND WAYLAND'S SMITHY

7¾ miles (12.5 km)

Beginning at the car park where Ashbury Hill crosses the Ridgeway, walk along the Ridgeway in a south-westerly direction. In about 200 yards, at the next crossing of tracks, turn left towards Red Barn and follow the track as it skirts to the west of Hailey Wood, Middle Wood and Upper Wood. Ashdown House **22** can be seen to the left of the track in Ashdown Park past Middle Wood. Built in the late 1600s, it was described by Pevsner as the 'perfect doll's house', and one can see why. It is now owned by the National Trust and is open from April to the end of October, on Wednesday and Saturday afternoons only. The woods are open all year, except Fridays.

Continue southwards past the end of Upper Wood for about 220 yards and take the path to the left. At the next crossing of tracks turn left again. Turn left on to the road and, after about half a mile (1 km), almost opposite a road leading to Ashdown Farm, strike right across the field and up Weathercock Hill. Follow the path, initially due east and then north-east, until a crossing of tracks, then turn left and continue back to the Ridgeway. Turn left again and, passing Wayland's Smithy **18** on the right, continue along the Ridgeway back to the car park. Oxfordshire County Council's leaflet *Ridgeway Walks: Ashdown House–Wayland's Smithy* has further details.

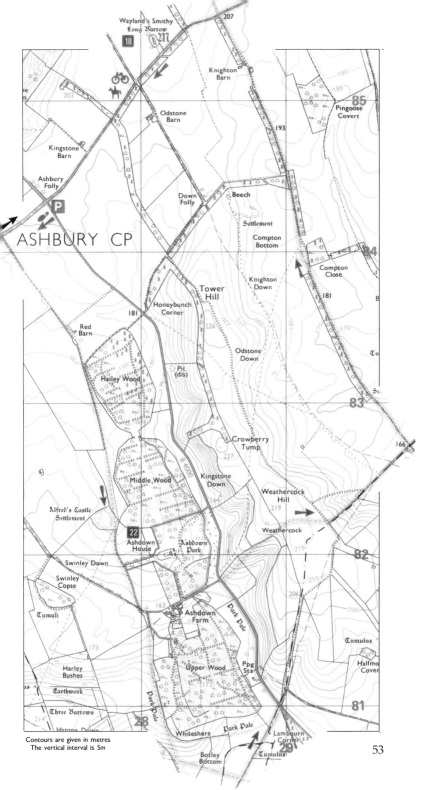

Wayland's Smithy
Long Barrow
207
18
Knighton
Barn
190
185
85
Pingoose
Covert
Odstone
Barn
203
193
Kingstone
Barn
Ashbury
Folly
P
Down
Folly
Beech
Compton
Close
84
181
ASHBURY CP
Settlement
Compton
Bottom
Tower
Hill
Knighton
Down
181
Honeybunch
Corner
Red
Barn
181
Odstone
Down
185
170
83
Hailey Wood
Pit
(dis)
166
Crowberry
Tump
227
Weathercock
Hill
Middle Wood
Kingstone
Down
219
Alfred's Castle
Settlement
Weathercock
82
Ashdown
House
22
Ashdown
Park
215
210
Swinley Down
206
200
Swinley
Copse
163
Tumuli
Ashdown
Farm
Park Pale
Tumulus
Halfmo
Cover
81
173
Harley
Bushes
Upper Wood
Ppg
Sta
Earthwork
Three Barrows
Park Pale
Idstone Down
28
29
Whiteshere
Park Pale
Lambourn
Corner
Tumulus
Botley
Bottom

Contours are given in metres
The vertical interval is 5m

53

Between the Smithy and Knighton Hill, less than 400 yards to the north-east along the Ridgeway, another line of trees nears the track, and Whitehorse Hill **20** with the ramparts of Uffington Castle **19** hill fort come into view. At the road, Wayland's Smithy is clearly signposted, as is the Ridgeway in both directions. Simply cross the road and continue along the broad track towards Whitehorse Hill which seems to dominate the view ahead.

The ascent from the road at Knighton Hill begins gently at first and then steepens sharply near Uffington Castle, taking you from about 680 feet (207 metres) to just over 820 feet (250 metres), a climb of some 140 feet (43 metres) in just over a mile (under 2 km). The fort ridge terminating in the scarp of Uffington Hill cuts across the Ridgeway path in front of you. About 600 yards before reaching the castle itself, the Ridgeway passes yet another road/track. This leads north to the Woolstone Hill car park and south to Lambourn (about 5 miles/8 km away). The Ridgeway soon passes to the south of Uffington Castle, situated on land owned now by the National Trust, although the castle itself is an English Heritage site. Just after you reach the top of the hill, there is a stile over the fence which leads to the ramparts of the castle where the trig point for Whitehorse Hill is clearly visible.

Do make the short diversion to the castle's ramparts – it is well worth it. Like many of the hill forts, Uffington Castle has a rich and varied flora, despite the thousands of feet trampling all over it! The ramparts support orchids, candytuft and field fleawort, in addition to the more common chalk downland species. The trackside verge of the Ridgeway itself has, from late spring to early autumn, a profusion of flowers, such as scabious, knapweed, several species of vetch, and a variety of grasses. Many of these are particularly attractive to butterflies. Chalkhill Blue, Small Blue, Gatekeeper, Ringlet and Marbled White can all be found in this area.

Although the ramparts of Uffington Castle are now much eroded, there is still evidence of an outer bank, a ditch and an inner bank. From the trig point the views all around, but especially to the north, are spectacular.

The White Horse **21** can be reached by making for the thorn bushes to the north of the trig point, then bearing right along the contour path. The hill figure is just below the signs asking you to avoid walking on it – there has been much unnecessary erosion in recent years. From the top, the shape is not readily discernible – you need to go a mile or two to the north and look back! But the magnificent contours of The Manger, nestling beneath the horse's head, are clearly visible – a truly splendid example of a dry valley formed by a melting glacier in the Ice Ages. To return to the Ridgeway, either double back to the hill fort or, if you do not mind missing out a hundred yards or so of the Ridgeway, go eastwards to the field boundary, and then follow it southwards to a stile in the corner. On the other side is the Ridgeway.

The villages of Uffington and Woolstone lie to the north of Whitehorse Hill and there are car parks on Woolstone Hill and at the foot of Uffington Castle (for the disabled and elderly only).

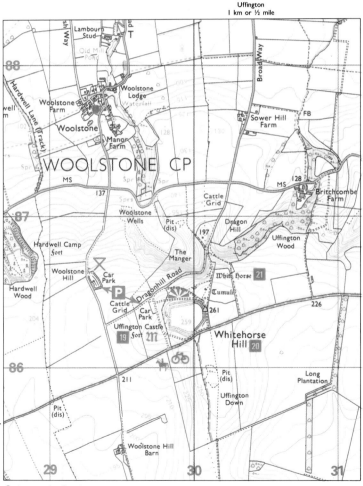

Uffington
1 km or ½ mile

Contours are given in metres
The vertical interval is 5m

The Iron Age hill forts

One of the most notable features of a journey along the Ridgeway is the line of earthworks, above all Barbury Castle **6**, Liddington **14**, Uffington **19** and Segsbury **29**, which occupy prominent points of high ground especially on the Wessex ridge.

The official plaque briefly informing visitors to Uffington Castle of its origins and history describes it as a '. . . hill fort defended by a bank and ditch with an entrance on the west and built during the Iron Age, 300 BC to AD 43'. It is obviously very hard to date a structure such as a hill fort. One way is by dating artefacts, such as tools, weapons or pottery which might be uncovered during excavation of the structure. So, if you find something which is clearly of Iron Age origin in the ditch which forms part of the castle defences, you know that the ditch must have been there first because an object cannot be deposited in something which does not exist! On the other hand, you do not know how long the structure had been there *before* the object was deposited in it. But, if no earlier objects are found, then it seems reasonable to assume that the structure must be more or less contemporaneous with what you have found.

As J.R.L. Anderson points out, however, common sense would suggest that all the hill forts along the Ridgeway were elements of a common strategic, defensive structure and that their location must mean that their original purpose was to defend the Ridgeway – an important line of communication – against attack from the north. As he goes on to suggest, such a tactic would have required considerable organisation and strong leadership. This would have been hard to find during the Iron Age period preceding the arrival of the Romans. There was, however, an earlier culture capable of organisation on such a scale. During the Bronze Age people would have no reason to defend the Ridgeway from the south but they *could* have had a need to defend it from unknown marauders from the north in much the same way that, in later times, the Romans built Hadrian's Wall to defend their colony against attack from the untamed lands in Scotland.

Of course, once such structures have been built, they obviously do not fall overnight and it is quite possible that people of a later age made use of them. J.R.L. Anderson's view does seem to make more strategic and political sense than the theory which stems from simple archaeological investigation.

Uffington Castle, one of the many Iron Age hill forts along the Ridgeway.

Perhaps we shall never know which argument is correct but it may be that, as dating methods improve, the truth will emerge. In the meantime, however, it is enough to marvel at the skill and effort that went into building fortresses that are still evident today, more than 2,000 years later.

Wayland's Smithy **18**

The plaque in front of the barrow describes it as a Neolithic burial chamber in a long barrow edged with stones, built in about 2800 B C. Beneath the mound was found a smaller long barrow of an earlier date with burials in wooden chambers. On either side of the Smithy is a ditch marked by lines of trees. The main entrance cairn is marked by four large stones. Wayland was the magical smith god of the Saxons and local legend has it that, if you leave your horse, together with a suitable payment, by the tomb, the animal will have been reshod on your return the next day. But Saxon gods would not have been heard of here until more than 3,000 years after the barrow was built. Access to Wayland's Smithy is easy from Compton Beauchamp and Knighton via Knighton Hill.

4 Whitehorse Hill to Wantage

via Sparsholt Firs
6¼ miles (10.2 km)

Note that the distance given above is from the summit of Whitehorse Hill and Uffington Castle to the point where the Ridgeway route crosses Manor Road, which leads northwards into the town of Wantage. Anyone staying in Wantage or planning to make use of its facilities will have a road walk of just over 2 miles (about 3.5 km) into the town, although the Court Hill Ridgeway Centre, where there is a youth hostel and camping, is only 440 yards off the ridge down the same road.

Returning to the Ridgeway route from Uffington Castle **19** (and nearby car parks), and keeping the castle on your left-hand side, the way now takes you a little north of east and begins slowly to descend from the hill's highest point of 859 feet (261 metres) and, as you look ahead, the going seems to be undulating. On the south-eastern horizon, beyond a clump of trees, a radio mast rises up to provide an indication of the way ahead; in fact, the mast is about 440 yards off the path to the south. The line of trees which leads off from the Ridgeway, about 880 yards east of the summit of Whitehorse Hill, is known, for obvious reasons, as Long Plantation. Shortly after passing the plantation, the track begins to climb again and, a little further on, the rounded hill to the south of the way, known as Rams Hill, is indicated on the map as the site of yet another fort, but the plough seems to have removed all traces of it so far as can be seen from the Ridgeway. There are wide views to the north, with Uffington and Kingston Lisle lying on the plain.

A CIRCULAR WALK FROM SPARSHOLT FIRS

7¾ miles (12.5 km) (see maps on pages 59 and 61)

From the car park at Sparsholt Firs **26** on the B4001, walk westwards along the Ridgeway past Blowingstone Hill **23** and Rams Hill to Whitehorse Hill **20** itself. Just past the trig point to the right, turn sharp left on to Uffington Down. As you walk, notice the so-called Long Dyke which, through ploughing over hundreds of years, has become a sort of shallow man-made scarp and then a raised causeway which also marks the parish boundary. With gallops to the left, at the apex of a triangular

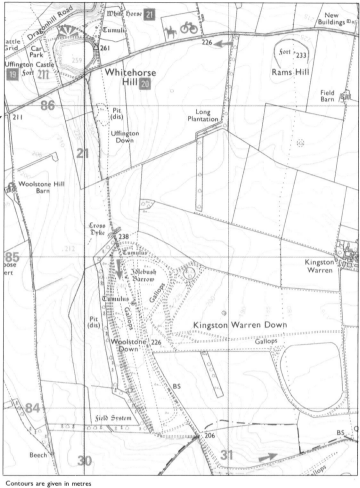

Contours are given in metres
The vertical interval is 5m

shaped line of trees, follow the track to the left and then right. A track then turns to the left although the gallops continue southwards. Turn left, towards Crog Hill. At Crog Hill follow the track to the right and then take the next left to join the minor road. Turn right on to the road and walk past Sevenbarrows House on the right. Just past Lambourn Seven Barrows, take the track to the left and follow it until it emerges on to the B4001. Turn left and follow the road back to the car park. Further details are in Oxfordshire County Council's leaflet: *Ridgeway Walks: Whitehorse Hill–Lambourn Seven Barrows*.

Having passed Rams Hill, the track begins to swing south-wards and before the next hill ahead can be seen the road leading to Kingston Lisle, about three-quarters of a mile (1.25 km) to the north down Blowingstone Hill **23**. There is an 800-yard walk down the road to look at the Blowing Stone in the garden of a cottage. If one blows into one of the holes which pierce the stone, one can produce a deep, trumpet-like sound. King Alfred may have put it to use during the Battle of Ashdown.

From the Ridgeway, and situated just to the south of the village, can be seen Kingstone Lisle House **24**, a fine Georgian house set in parkland. It is open to the public on Thursdays and bank holiday weekends between Easter and early September.

The road which the Ridgeway crosses at this point joins the B4001 in the south and, in about 5 miles (8 km), leads to the village of Lambourn. About $2\frac{1}{2}$ miles (4 km) from the Ridgeway, down the road towards Lambourn, is the spectacular group of tumuli known as the Seven Barrows **25**, although there must have been something like thirty different kinds of barrows here before farming took its toll. Even now, more than seven are visible. To the south of the Ridgeway, the views now are rather restricted but do include the attractive rolling downland which typifies this part of Oxfordshire. The top of the hill is reached at a height of 743 feet (226 metres) and, to the right of the track, there is a group of trees called Hillbarn Clump. Between Collett Bush and Wixen Bush (which presumably had some signifi-cance at one time to warrant being named on the map), the track climbs. There is very little depth of soil here, and the profusion of chalk-loving plants will delight the summer visitor. The track runs south-eastwards again, climbing to a height of some 794 feet (242 metres) before it levels out.

At this point a track to the right leads to Hill Barn; there is a drinking water tap at this junction. You are now approaching Sparsholt Firs **26**, which, despite their name, seem to consist almost entirely of deciduous trees. Just before you arrive at the plantation itself, the Ridgeway route joins a metalled road from Sparsholt $1\frac{1}{2}$ miles (2.4 km) to the north. Bear right on to the road and, where it joins the B4001, continue straight ahead on to the broad Ridgeway track. To the south of the track, looking back a little, are the Lambourn Downs, and on the north of the path adjacent to the gallops there is a highly favoured area for flying model aircraft. By all means stop and watch from the Ridgeway, but please note that this is private land – the model aircraft club has permission to use the gallops.

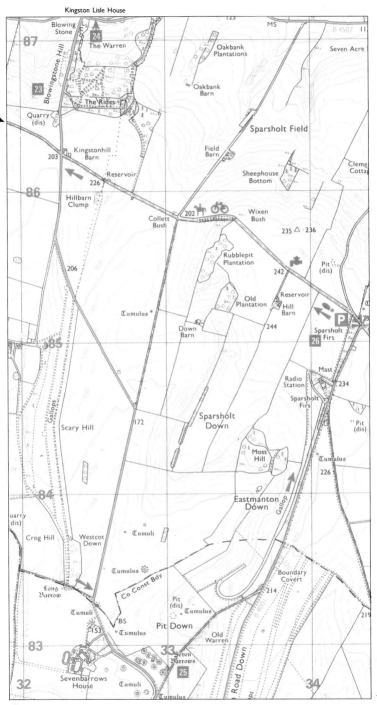

Kingston Lisle House

Blowing Stone

The Warren

Oakbank Plantations

Seven Acre

Blowingstone Hill

Oakbank Barn

The Rides

Sparsholt Field

Quarry (dis)

Kingstonhill Barn

Field Barn

Clemp Cottag

203

Sheephouse Bottom

Reservoir

226

Wixen Bush

Hillbarn Clump

202

235 △ ·236

Collett Bush

Rubblepit Plantation

Pit (dis)

206

242

Old Plantation

Reservoir

Hill Barn

Tumulus

Down Barn

244

Sparsholt Firs

Radio Station

Mast

·234

Gallops

Scary Hill

172

Sparsholt Down

Sparsholt Firs

Pit (dis)

Moss Hill

Tumulus

226

Eastmanton Down

Gallop

uarry (dis)

Crog Hill

Westcot Down

Tumuli

Long Barrow

Tumulus

Boundary Covert

214

Co Const Bdy

Pit (dis)

Tumulus

219

Tumuli

BS

153

Tumulus

Pit Down

Old Warren

Road Down

Sevenbarrows

Seven Barrows

Sevenbarrows House

Tumuli

Tumulus

Contours are given in metres
The vertical interval is 5m

61

The countryside in this area is open and pleasing, with panoramic views in most directions. You travel south-eastwards at first, passing another Hackpen Hill to the left, and then, as the way bears eastwards again, a line of racehorse gallops accompanies the route for about a mile (1.5 km). The unploughed, formerly rabbit-cropped turf of these areas is now carefully managed by private owners to provide large gallops with soft, springy turf on which to train racehorses, with little fear of injury to these highly bred and very expensive animals.

Through the valley to the north-east can be seen the village of Letcombe Bassett **27** about half a mile (1 km) north of the Ridgeway, which takes you across a metalled road known as Gramp's Hill. If, at Gramp's Hill **28**, you look back in the direction from which you have just come, the natural cut into the hillside, known as the Devil's Punchbowl, can clearly be seen. Cross the road and continue on the more or less level track which, at this point, becomes rather sticky again. Any views are restricted by hedges and small trees. About 880 yards after leaving the road, a track leads off to the right, marked by a circular route symbol of an arrow with 'CR' inside it, used to mark Oxfordshire County Council's walks, and passes

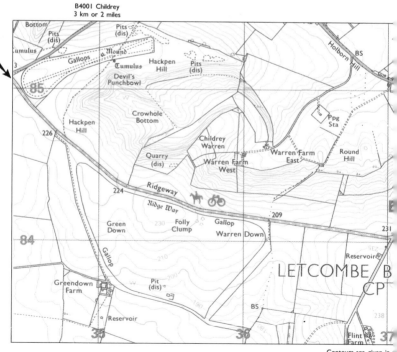

Contours are given in
The vertical interval

Parsonagehill Barn. Shortly after, a metalled track to the left, known as Smith's Hill, leads down to the Letcombes and here there is another circular route indicated – the way to the right, however, is private. In about 100 yards there is another footpath heading downhill to the left, signposted to Letcombe Bassett which is about half a mile (1 km) to the north. This track, too, forms part of the Wantage circular walk.

Now the Ridgeway begins to descend towards what appears on the map as the quite major earthwork of Segsbury or Letcombe Castle **29** fort to the north of the track. Opposite Segsbury Farm, a broad, grassy track is shown as a right of way to the fort. In fact, I found the 'castle' a rather disappointing ditch and bank. Much of it is now swathed in hawthorn bushes providing cover for a variety of birds and even deer. From here, you continue roughly eastwards until you reach Manor Road which leads down into the busy market town of Wantage.

For anyone continuing onwards, the signposts clearly indicate that you turn right on to the road and almost immediately left. Notice, however, that the Court Hill Ridgeway Centre **30** (see page 64) is signposted as a quarter of a mile (400 metres) to the left down Manor Road towards Wantage.

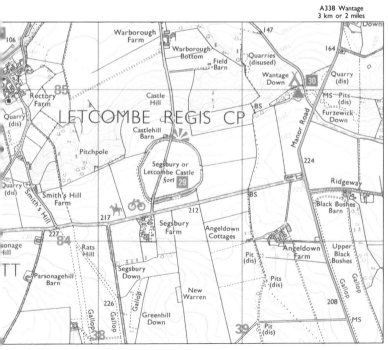

urs are given in metres
vertical interval is 5m

The Ridgeway Centre offers accommodation and field studies facilities.

The Ridgeway Centre

It may perhaps seem a little unusual to be including in a guide book to a rural national trail a special feature on a recently constructed facility which the trail offers but this is rather a unique situation.

Described in the official leaflet as '. . . a lively and exciting place to stay . . .' and located on Court Hill with fine views across the Vale of White Horse, the Ridgeway Centre **30** makes an ideal rest stop. The accommodation and other facilities have been developed around five disused barns from local farms that were dismantled and re-erected on the present site, which was originally a chalk pit and became the Wantage rubbish tip. The site has now a new lease of life and the Centre has two holiday flats, a display and field studies area, a camping site, a barbecue area, the usual kitchen and dining room, superior

grade and standard grade youth hostel accommodation and even a swimming pool.

The Centre was sponsored mainly by the Vale of White Horse District Council, Countryside Commission, Thames and Chilterns Tourist Board, Ernest Cook Trust, Wantage Town Council, Oxfordshire County Council and the Toby Adcock Memorial Fund. These organisations should be congratulated for their far-sightedness in promoting such a centre. Dr Dick Squires, a local GP, also deserves a mention. Having thought of the idea of a hostel on the Downs, he set about raising the funds and was involved in the project from start to finish.

Anyone wishing to stay at the Centre or to make enquiries about the facilities mentioned here, as well as a variety of others, should contact the Warden, The Court Hill Ridgeway Centre, Court Hill, Letcombe Regis, Nr Wantage, Oxfordshire, tel. Wantage (02357) 60253.

5 Wantage to Bury Down

past the Baron of Wantage Monument and Scutchamer Knob
5¾ miles (9.2 km)

It is worth bearing in mind that, if you have decided to stay the night in Wantage itself, unless you take a taxi to rejoin the Ridgeway, in the morning you will have a 2-mile (3.5-km) road walk uphill before you get back to the route. There is car parking at Manor Road, however.

Crossing Manor Road, turn right and immediately left to resume your eastward journey. The countryside on either side of the Ridgeway is still typical of modern farming methods although the view to the south, through the hedgerow, is much pleasanter.

The route begins to climb upwards a little after a group of houses and, at the brow of the hill, there is a large, black-painted barn. Over the hill, and down again; the metalling on the track begins to peter out while the views ahead to the east start to open up. Pass the buildings of Whitehouse Farm on your left.

At the point where the track takes a sharp turn to the left (north) there is a small coniferous plantation edged by some young beech trees. After about 100 yards you come to a T-junction.

The Ridgeway turns sharply to the south-east here but for travellers from the east, another sign indicates a short cut to Court Hill Ridgeway Centre **30**. The way now becomes the typical, broad, rutted, chalky grass track pointing in the direction of a radio mast ahead. The shape of the hill here is such that the views to the north are somewhat restricted although, to the south-west, the broad expanses of open farmland, here and there dotted with patches of woodland, persist. Over the farmland, the tinkling songs of skylarks spiralling upwards mix with the 'pee-wit' calls of the lapwings to add a little musical colour to the scene.

The B4494 road from Wantage comes into view but, before it is reached, the track forks. One is tempted to continue straight on to the south-east but, in fact, the route follows the left-hand fork.

The Ordnance Survey map informs you that here, in 1872, bronze palstaves, which are axe heads designed to fit into split wooden handles, were found. Today in the fields to the left is a major piggery, marked 'Minimal Disease, Camborough Hybrid Pigs'. I wonder what the Ridgeway was like when it was first being used as a trading route; with such farming methods in evidence and with modern roads in sight, too, it is hard to imagine, although this can be a good place to stop for coffee, sheltered by isolated trees and bushes. Somewhere, a hidden cock pheasant croaked out its harsh, unmusical call on a cold April day.

Approaching the road, the Ridgeway becomes a gravelled farm track once again and, at the crossing, there is ample car parking space. Simply cross the road and continue journeying

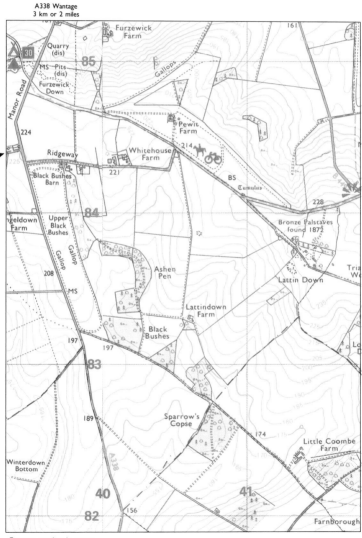

Contours are given in metres
The vertical interval is 5m

Furzewick Down is typical of the landscape to be seen on this section of the Ridgeway.

north-eastwards. Do not be tempted to take the metalled track forking left. In the distance, the spike of a monument comes into view, built 'on the Site of a Tumulus', according to the map. At this point, you are following part of the circular walk described on page 72, and to the left is Middlehill Down. The route is a broad grassy track and, in April, I saw three hares playing in the fields to the right. Rather sadder, however, was a stained and battered notice dated 21st June 1987, 5 p.m. – apparently a cocker spaniel bitch had been lost, and I wondered if she had ever been found again. It was, though, a salutary warning for Ridgeway walkers to keep their dogs under control, especially as I heard the crack of shotguns and the wingflaps of many pigeons rising into the air.

From close to, the monument **31** looks smaller than it appears from the distance. On its square concrete plinth, the circular, concrete-cross-topped column of a monument to the soldier and Victoria Cross holder, Robert Loyd-Lindsay, Baron of Wantage, is hardly an attractive affair, erected as it was by the Baron's wife. On the other hand, as the tree cover begins to increase all around, the scenery gains interest and, from the density of hoofprints in the mud, this is obviously a popular route for horseriders.

In the late 19th century, Lord Wantage and his descendants planted a large number of scattered copses and shelterbelts, mainly of beech, elm and oak. In the present century, a phase of softwood planting brought the total area of woodland on the estate to about 1,000 acres (400 hectares). The contribution to the landscape made by this planting can readily be appreciated. The value of the woods for timber is supplemented by that of game rearing, and the land certainly creates the impression that it is well-husbanded, as partridges fly off from the long grass when you near a small plantation of conically shaped evergreens. The Ridgeway route bears slightly to the right with the curious little plantation on the left; other tracks here are 'Private, Keep Out'! A little to the east of the plantation by Ridgeway Down, there is a drinking water tap on the left-hand edge of the way. Also to the left is another curious stand of trees, this time circular, to the north of which is Midsummer Wood and Ardington Down. With the broad track climbing gently, and with very comfortable going underfoot, the route takes a slight turn to the north and, about 275 yards past the tap, the Oxfordshire Circular Walk bears off sharply to the right, descending between two woods.

As you reach the brow of the hill, to the left of the Ridgeway there is an odd-looking, fenced square construction, which I suspect was a reservoir. After this, another plantation stands on the left and there are tracks crossing to left and right before it. Just behind the fence on the north-west corner of this junction will be found a small sarsen stone bearing a plaque in memory of Lady Penelope Betjeman, wife of Sir John, the late Poet Laureate. The Betjemans lived at various times at Uffington, Wantage and Farnborough, and often walked the Ridgeway. From here, it is possible to reach the villages of Lockinge and Ardington **32** about 2½ miles (4 km) to the north (see page 74).

It was here on the Ridgeway that a seemingly endless stream of motorcyclists passed me as they rode in the opposite direction to mine. At first, I was irritated by their presence but it must be admitted that they had as much right to be there as I did, and each of them could not have been more considerate. Shortly after the woodland, there is another crossing of paths although, this time, only the route to the north is a public right of way, heading first for East Ginge, from where East Hendred can be reached if you fancy a 3-mile (5-km) hike out of your way.

Approaching the top of the hill, with its stand of pine trees to the right, in the distance to the north of east the rather untidy sprawl of Harwell Laboratory (formerly the Atomic Energy Research Establishment, set up in 1946) comes into view.

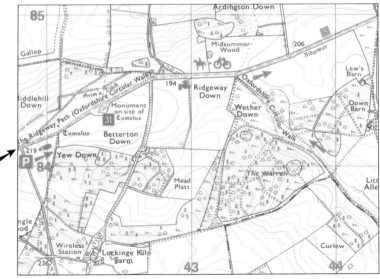

Contours are given in metres
The vertical interval is 5m

To the left now is East Ginge Down, and ahead is the top of Cuckhamsley Hill at 668 feet (203 metres), picked out by a stand of trees. On reaching them, I saw they were surrounded by a broken fence and marked 'Private', although the landowner has provided a stile leading into the trees. I could discern in the dim light among the trees what is marked on the map only as 'tumulus' but which is Scutchamer Knob **33**. It is a curious affair. It looks as though once it may have been a round barrow but it now is a semi-circular bank with no front. It appears to have been vandalised by those who believed it held a hoard of treasure.

Opinions seem to differ as to the name 'Scutchamer'. It may have been derived from Cwicchelmshlaew, the burial place of the Saxon king, Cwicchelm, who died in A D 593, but Anderson claims that a 'scutcher' was someone who 'scutched' or beat out the flax after it had been retted or soaked to loosen the fibres, and that this was the place where local villagers once came to hold their fairs.

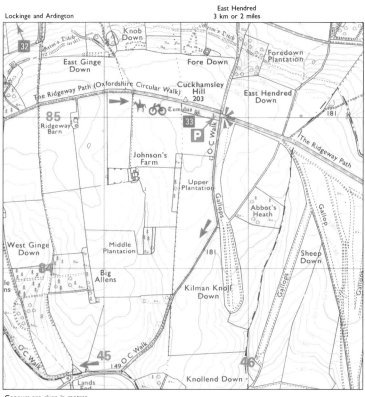

Conours are given in metres
The vertical interval is 5m

Onward, and again there are gallops to the right of the Ridgeway. After another 880 yards or so, two more rights of way lead off to the left, the first to the north passing by the perimeter of Harwell Laboratory and the second heading north-east to Chilton. Your way continues straight ahead, a little to the south of east, with the Chilton Downs to the left, Cow Down to the right, and your destination for this section of the route, Bury Down, straight ahead. The views to the north are broad and sweeping. On your left now, the A34 trunk road strides, a broad, grey stripe across the green downland with the Central Electricity Generating Board's Didcot Power Station on its left.

Didcot Power Station was built on the site of an old Army Central Ordnance Depot and cost £100 million to build. The first unit came into operation in 1970, and it now has four 500-megawatt generators driven by solid fuel. Most power stations of comparable size have eight of the giant cooling towers which make Didcot such a landmark but here there are only six, apparently to '. . . minimise their impact on the surrounding area. . .' Be that as it may, in certain lights the towers do have a kind of eerie charm. Interestingly, too, part of the site has been turned into a field study centre and nature trail for children, for which the station received the 1970 Countryside Award.

On Bury Down **34**, where there is ample car parking space, the Ridgeway crosses a minor road leading in a southerly direction to the village of West Ilsley **35**. To the north, in about half a mile (1 km), the road joins the busy A34.

A CIRCULAR WALK TO SCUTCHAMER KNOB
6 miles (10 km) (see maps on pages 70 and 71)

Start at the car park where the B4494, Chainhill Road from Wantage, crosses the Ridgeway. Follow the Ridgeway eastwards past the monument **31** and Scutchamer Knob **33** to the point past Cuckhamsley Hill where the minor road from East Hendred reaches the Ridgeway. Here turn right as directed on to the Oxfordshire Circular Walk and follow the walk past gallops on the left. Continue on the circular walk until it swings back to rejoin the Ridgeway between Wether Down and Ridgeway Down. Turn left and return to the car park.

Further details are in Oxfordshire County Council's leaflet: *Ridgeway Walks: Monument–Scutchamer Knob–West Ginge Down.*

Scutchamer Knob, probably once a barrow.

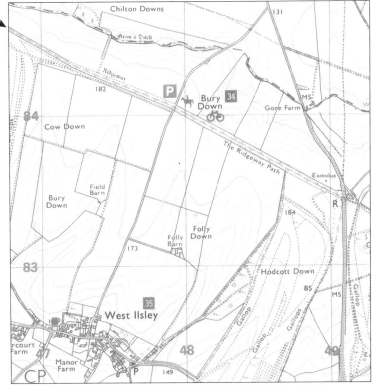

Lockinge and Ardington

The abandonment of the hamlet of Snap (see page 47) is a salutary reminder of what can happen to a country village when there are no jobs for the residents. The same fate could have befallen the villages of Lockinge and Ardington **32**, near Wantage. Their population fell drastically after 1950 since the Lockinge Estate, both employer and landowner, was unable to provide enough jobs on its increasingly mechanised farmland.

Then in the early 1970s, Christopher Loyd, the estate owner, and his agent decided to do something practical to save the villages. Redundant farm buildings were used to house small businesses and craft workshops, which provide more than 100 jobs for residents of the area, and a village housing trust has renovated old cottages and built new homes, particularly for the elderly and young people, both of whom usually lose out in the village housing market. A local enterprise scheme links Ardington and Lockinge with three neighbouring villages, so the efforts in one area can spread further afield. Instead of becoming a backwater of decaying houses, or a commuter's oasis totally depopulated except at weekends, the villages are facing a more certain future and are unlikely to become the Snaps of the 21st century.

The memorial to Lord Wantage (1832–1901), who built a model farm and village on the Lockinge estate.

Today the Home Farm houses a craft centre as well as other small businesses.

75

6 Bury Down to Streatley

past Compton and Aldworth
8¼ miles (13.4 km)

This part of the Ridgeway is popular with walkers, horseriders and motorcyclists in all seasons and in all weathers. It is somehow encouraging to think that it is still a busy green road even if its use is for pleasure rather than necessity. And there is good countryside to the north-east with rolling, open downland and the occasional clump of trees breaking up the line of the horizon. From here to Streatley is just about my favourite stretch of the western Ridgeway but there is just one feature which mars this end of its length: it seems impossible to escape the traffic noise from the A 34. Most of us use roads such as this one very regularly and, as we speed along, insulated from most of the engine and tyre noise, we scarcely think of the disturbance to the countryside and its inhabitants. Nevertheless, busy roads do have their advantages for some kinds of wildlife; kestrels, for example, seem to favour them as happy hunting grounds.

Before reaching the A 34, a public right of way to West Ilsley **35** leaves the Ridgeway in a southerly direction; it is part of a Berkshire County Council recreational route (see page 78) and is marked with the county's crest of a crown above two lions.

Even though you have crossed roads earlier along the Ridgeway, somehow it seems odd to be approaching such a major arterial road as the A 34. The route to take is clearly indicated, however, by red arrows and acorn marker posts, and you are led on to a gravel track and a concrete tunnel which passes beneath the road. At this point, you are about 1½ miles (2.5 km) from East Ilsley; there is, in fact, a public right of way heading southwards from here, too. It is also possible to get to East Ilsley **36** via a number of tracks, particularly where the route bears a little more to the south and approaches to within just over a mile (1.75 km) of the centre of the village, which was once famous for its sheep fairs (see page 84).

With the A 34 left behind, and with an easterly wind blowing, the noise from the road becomes less intrusive. Immediately you emerge from the tunnel there is a bridlepath to the right but you go straight ahead to the south-east where, after another 100 yards, a gallop runs southwards into the downs and woodlands.

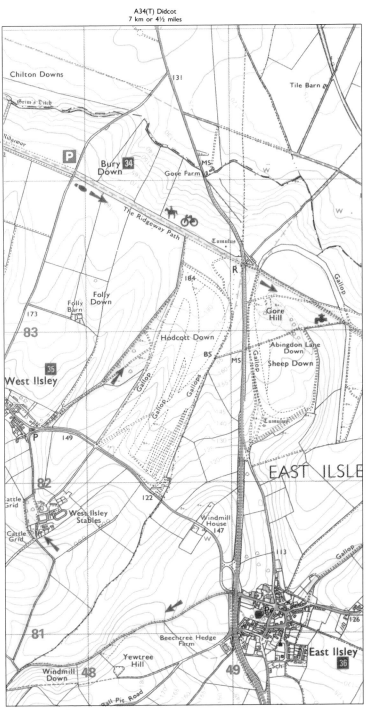

Chilton Downs

131

Tile Barn

Grim's Ditch

Ridgeway

P Bury 34
Down

MS

Gore Farm

W

The Ridgeway Path

W

Tumulus

R

184

Gallop

Folly
Down

Gore
Hill

Folly
Barn

173

Abingdon Lane
Down

83

Hodcott Down

BS

Sheep Down

MS

Gallop

West Ilsley 35

Gallop

Gallop

Gallops

P 149

Tumulus

EAST ILSLE

82

Cattle
Grid

122

West Ilsley
Stables

Windmill
House
147

113

Gallop

Cattle
Grid

W

81

126

Beechtree Hedge
Farm

East Ilsley 36

Yewtree
Hill

Sch

Windmill
Down 48

49

Ball Pit Road

Contours are given in metres
The vertical interval is 5m

77

Just before the summit of Several Down **37** – marked with a trig point just off to the right – there is a welcome drinking water tap by the side of the track. The going underfoot here is not easy and full of deep ruts. Shortly beyond Several Down, yet another gallop leaves the Ridgeway to the south, as well as a bridleway or recreational route, and a little after these there is a north-heading bridleway. The views to the north are delightful. Sparsely scattered lines of trees, like rows of shaving brushes, punctuate the landscape. At the point where the lane from Ilsley Barn Farm merges with the Ridgeway, the route also becomes a concrete lane and, about 330 yards further on, yet another bridleway crosses it. Another 330 yards or so brings you to one more bridleway which crosses the concrete lane. Do not be tempted to continue straight on along the road. To the right, the bridleway heads once more into East Ilsley while the road ahead leads to Superity Farm and then to Compton **38**, where there is a research establishment of the Agricultural and Food Research Council's Institute for Animal Health.

A CIRCULAR WALK TO EAST ILSLEY
5½ miles (9 km) (see maps on pages 77 and 79)

Begin at the parking space on the Ridgeway at Bury Down **34** where the minor road from West Ilsley **35** crosses the Ridgeway. Follow the Ridgeway in a south-easterly direction under the A 34 trunk road and continue on past the trig point on Several Down. Turn right at the next circular route waymark and follow some gallops into East Ilsley **36**. Where the track meets the road, turn right and continue straight through the village heading roughly east, passing again under the A 34. Notice the winding mechanism of the disused village well by the duck pond. Look, too, at the 13th century Church of St Mary and the Hall and Kennet House. You will come to another waymark directing you towards Windmill Down. About 1¼ miles (2 km) from the A 34, turn sharp right and then right again. After about 880 yards the way turns left and passes West Ilsley Stables which are on your right. Follow the metalled road to the eastern outskirts of West Ilsley. Turn right on to a minor road and then soon after fork left on to a route returning you to the Ridgeway. Turn left and return to the car park.

Further details of this walk are in Berkshire County Council's leaflet: *East/West Ilsley Circular Walk.*

The route now turns sharp left heading in a north-easterly direction and returning to partly rutted, partly grassy, partly chalky track – typical Ridgeway. Compton Downs are to your left and, on either side, the rolling downland stretches away into the distance. On reaching the valley bottom, the Ridgeway is lined with trees. There is a bridleway to Compton which is only 1½ miles (2.5 km) from the Ridgeway. (Please notice the 'No camping' signs by the bridleway.) Over a bridge, and the line of a dismantled railway is clearly marked by trees, fences, and the original cutting. From here you can see the Ridgeway snaking up the hillside ahead as a creamy white track, which can be slippery in wet weather. A footpath leads off to the left but your way continues straight on, ascending gently at first but then

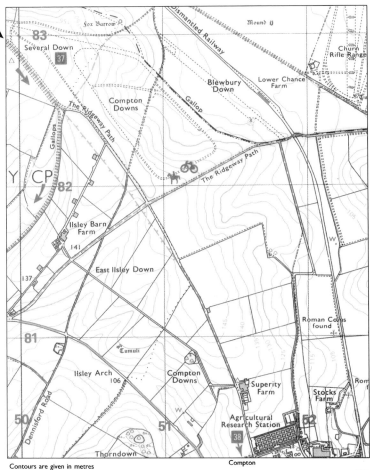

Contours are given in metres
The vertical interval is 5m

Compton

79

more steeply. In 440 yards, just after the point where a bridleway joins from the north-west and where there are gallops and a rifle range to the left, the track forks. Take the right fork as the signpost indicates, and head south-east once more. In the area directly to the east of the fork, there is the site of a Roman temple on Lowbury Hill, but you pass south of it and nothing can be seen bar the hill itself.

This is fine downland and, in April, the sheep may be bleating in the fields over which the lapwings wheel and call, while pigeons coo from the isolated copses. Halfway up the next rise, there is a small copse and a criss-crossing of a number of tracks leading to Compton, Lowbury Hill, and the largish village of Blewbury some 2½ miles (4 km) away. After another 550 yards and two-thirds of the way up the next slope, there is another 'crossroads' with tracks going off to right and left, but with the route straight ahead marked Ridgeway Path. Very shortly after, the path forks again, and the Ridgeway follows the left fork slightly south of east. To the right is the village of Aldworth **39** where the church with its great stone effigies, the 'Aldworth Giants', is well worth a look and where there is an excellent pub, The Bell, but to get there would mean quite a diversion.

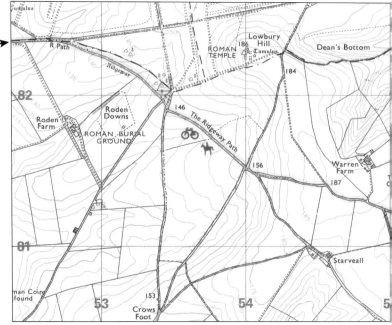

Contours are given in
The vertical interval

As I walked along one April, courting yellowhammers were so preoccupied with their own pursuits that they seemed not to be aware of my presence as they flew, beak to tail, ahead of me. After a further quite steep climb of about 33 yards the going eases and begins to level out. From here it is more or less downhill all the way to Streatley; and soon the Goring gap comes into view. This beautiful, comparatively narrow gorge-like cutting in the Thames breaks through the chalk ridge in a north-west to south-east direction. To the right the impressive hollow of Streatley Warren **40** stretches out in a most attractive vista with the green- and straw-coloured slopes dotted with isolated trees and small copses. Do not be tempted to take the track into the woods unless you have time for a walk. There is a delightful gamekeeper's cottage, which sometimes has teas available, just at the entrance to Town Copse and, if you were to continue along that way, you would pass through the very well-kept Well Barn Estate, eventually reaching the A 417 Blewbury Road. Returning to the Ridgeway, continue to the bottom of the steepest part of the descent, close to another Warren Farm. Here the way becomes a metalled lane, and there is car parking space for perhaps a dozen cars.

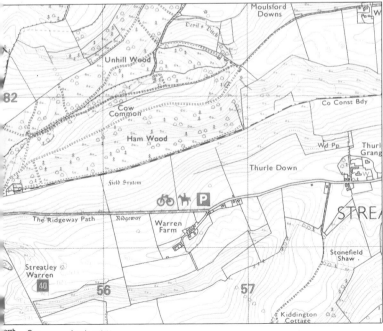

Continue on down the lane for about 1½ miles (2.5 km) past a charming wooden cottage with its brick-built chimney stack, and Thurle Grange with its newly developed housing. Now Goring and Streatley Golf Course comes into view on the right and a public footpath, in fact marked as the Old Ridgeway, crosses it to join the B4009 road just west of Streatley, but the actual Ridgeway Path continues along the road, eventually reaching the A417. Pass the rather grand-looking clubhouse and then, just before reaching the road, there is the entrance on the right to the National Trust property of Lough Down which is open to the public.

Turn right on to the A417 (if you are travelling westwards, the lane from the A417 to the Ridgeway is marked Rectory Road). A little further on, where the road joins the A329, turn right again into the main village of Streatley **41** on the west bank of the River Thames. The two main roads meet at a dangerous corner; it is best to cross to the eastern side of the A417 *before* crossing to the eastern side of the A329. Just before the traffic lights, there is a bus stop where you can catch buses to Oxford or Reading (there is no Sunday service). Anyone wishing to stay overnight in the youth hostel should continue past the traffic lights for some 55 yards where it will be found on the right-hand side of the road.

For those who are staying in Goring **42**, on the other side of the river, or who are continuing along the Ridgeway, turn left at the traffic lights down the hill towards the Thames. Before you reach the river, on the left-hand side of the road, there is an attractive church with a square, flint, perhaps Norman tower. This is the Parish Church of St Mary at Streatley-on-Thames in the diocese of Oxford. The church was built in the 13th century although there was probably a place of worship on the present site in Saxon times and relics of Roman origin have been found in the churchyard. Apart from the tower, the church was rebuilt in 1864 although elements of the older building have been retained. On the little road leading to the church, another attractive building is the malthouse.

The official boundary separating Streatley from Goring is just before the first of the two bridges crossing the Thames. On the left is the rather grand, and much extended, Swan Hotel with its moored boats and floating function rooms. This spot is very popular with tourists in summer. There is also the rather curious, red-brick, probably Victorian creation of a village hall with its pagoda-like clock tower. If you are unfamiliar with

Oxfordshire and its breweries, it is well worth sampling Brakspeare's Ales, which are brewed in Henley-on-Thames, in one of the attractive pubs, such as the John Barleycorn or the riverside Old Leatherne Bottle.

The Thames Path will eventually meet the Ridgeway at Streatley, and continue to Wallingford up the western side of the river.

Contours are given in metres
The vertical interval is 5m

A sheep fair at East Ilsley c. 1906.

East Ilsley sheep fairs

The village of East Ilsley **36** used to be called 'Market Ilsley' because it was an important centre for sheep sales, being close to the Ridgeway and in a sheep-rearing area. Indeed, the first records of sheep fairs at East Ilsley can be traced to medieval times; then in 1620 Sir Francis Moore, as lord of the manor, received a charter to hold a market for sheep and corn. Once or twice a month on Wednesdays from January to September the village was host to farmers from all over southern England. By the middle of the 18th century some 80,000 sheep could be penned in the village at the annual fairs, which were larger than

the Wednesday markets and made the village a hive of industry, supporting 13 public houses, many famed for their ale.

One local resident has clear childhood memories of the pre-First World War fairs and 'the different faces of the sheep; some black, some white and the round chubby faces of the lambs – but all with brown, expressionless eyes, no doubt longing to be away from East Ilsley and back on the downs in peace'. Shepherds would drive the sheep to East Ilsley from as far away as Salisbury, trekking across the downs, and it was really the coming of motorised transport that contributed to the decline of the fairs. The last great sheep fair was held in 1934; attempts to revive them in the 1970s were shortlived, however.

7 Streatley to Mongewell Park

through Goring on Thames, South Stoke and North Stoke
5½ miles (8.8 km)

About 100 yards after you have crossed the second of the two bridges between Streatley **41** and Goring **42**, turn left into Thames Road almost immediately opposite Goring village hall. Continue along this road to a footpath which you follow to another road. Turn left and continue straight ahead. Where the road turns sharply to the right and passes under a railway bridge, your route goes straight ahead.

Here, the Ridgeway is sandwiched between the Thames to the left and the railway line. The path comes out on to a road which leads down to the Old Leatherne Bottle public house. Head for South Stoke **43**, with a small sailing dinghy park and the boathouse of Goring on Thames Sailing Club on the left. There is a large, red-brick, Victorian property to the right and, at this point, the metalled road becomes a gravelled driveway once again. There are splendid lawns leading down to the river with its weeping willows and pleasure boats. In the trees all around there may be the harsh chiffchaff song from which the little brown warbler gets its name, as well as the descending melodic warble of the willow warbler.

As the driveway becomes a narrow dirt path again, it emerges into more open fields between the river and the railway line on the embankment to the right. On the left is a reed bed with an occasional willow leading down to the river which is picked out by a line of taller trees along its bank. On reaching the first houses of South Stoke, go left on to the road and pass another thatch-roofed pub, The Perch and Pike, and see ahead the tower of South Stoke Church with its Victorian schoolhouse.

The flint-built, but partly cement-rendered church of St Andrew was built in the 15th century but has been repaired and altered even as recently as the 1960s. In 1974 Oxfordshire Rural Community Council decided that the churchyard was worth an award. Further on, at the road junction, you turn left and head towards the river again. Here you part company with the Swan's Way, a 65-mile (105-km) long bridleway which runs from Goring on Thames to Salcey Forest in Northamptonshire.

The route goes over a little bridge, crossing a small stream, and there are reed beds to the right. At the end of the lane, turn right through a gate and on to the open river bank.

A329 Wallingford
5 km or 3 miles

Contours are given in metres
The vertical interval is 5m

5 km or 3 miles
A329 Pangbourne

Now follow the Thames, which winds roughly northwards, for nearly 2 miles (about 3 km) on soft, springy turf. Note the arches of Moulsford Railway Bridge **44**, built by Isambard Kingdom Brunel (1839), which are dramatically oblique, their brickwork having been ingeniously laid askew.

Half a mile (1 km) after the bridge turn right along a gravel drive towards some houses, turning left again where a signpost tells you North Stoke is three-quarters of a mile (1.2 km) distant. Now you are on another narrow dirt footpath. As I passed in April there were Canada geese honking out their sentry calls by the river and a green woodpecker yaffled in a nearby tree. Sitting on the ridges of the ploughed field was a pair of reed buntings, and pheasants revealed their presence by klaxon notes.

You come to a small concrete footbridge across a rivulet beyond which there is a stile. Over this, continue across the field to the stile on the other side. The path continues to be obvious with the houses of North Stoke **45** now appearing ahead. The path looks as though it wants to continue around the field but the way actually forks to the left across a stile marked with a yellow arrow. The path here is muddy, very narrow, lined with trees and with old, rather open woodland between it and the river. There are houses and gardens on the right. Cross another stile and now the flint tower of a church is visible and the footpath crosses over yet one more stile in a brick wall and into the churchyard. The path through the churchyard is obvious and leads to the path from the lych gate at the entrance.

Stop and look at the church. It has real charm and a feeling of great antiquity. There was a 7th century Saxon church on this site but even the comparatively 'modern' church which still stands was built in the mid-13th century. Among its many fascinating features are the rather faded wall paintings which date back to the 14th century. Photocopied sheets inside the church will give you more information on its history and architecture.

Leave the churchyard via the main path and the lych gate, but, before you finally depart, notice the sundial which was erected to those who served their country in the First World War. You come out on to a metalled road with Rectory Farmhouse on the left, via the village hall, or was it a church hall or schoolhouse perhaps, which was built in 1864. Buses to Reading and Wallingford run infrequently from the crossroads on the B4009 (no Sunday service).

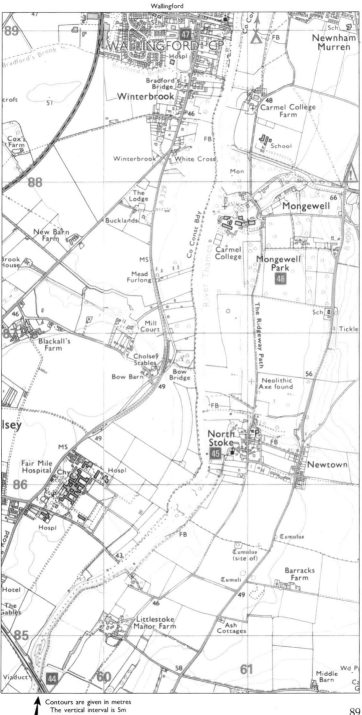

Contours are given in metres
The vertical interval is 5m

89

Continue along the village street past Brick Lodge and the Old Mill on the right. Cross the millstream and, eventually, the road peters out into a driveway. Carry straight on into a broad, rutted lane between fences and trees which soon becomes a track across a field with a hedge to the left. Continue straight on and do not be tempted to turn right towards the road.

Pass across a field boundary, and follow a bridleway which cuts a broad swathe through a field of rough grazing. On the left is a stand of old trees still surviving in the wet ground among marsh marigolds. You are in Mongewell Park **46** amid fenced fields and landscaped trees; the park is now occupied by Carmel College, a Jewish public school. Enter the grounds of the college past a car park and swimming pool on the left.

As you walk along the metalled road in the college grounds ignore paths leading left and right and continue straight ahead following the Ridgeway waymarks. Continue with the buildings on the left and stay on the road, so that the lake is on the right-hand side, and walk past a green-painted public telephone box with a post box outside it. Where the road turns sharp right keep straight on, bearing rightish, on to a bridleway heralded by a concrete bollard. Follow this paved path until just before it bears slightly to the right and its paving finishes. You cross a stile on the right into a narrow strip of woodland which follows the line of Grim's Ditch (see page 100) intermittently all the way to Nuffield. There are some buildings on the left as you head eastwards towards the A4074. You have just turned away from the public right of way that could take you to Wallingford **47**, $1\frac{1}{4}$ miles (2 km) away, if that is your destination.

Wallingford

Today, the busy but attractive Thames-side town of Wallingford **47** takes on a largely Georgian appearance, although recently there has been a little development near the centre and, on the outskirts, there are light industrial sites housing maltings. The history of Wallingford reaches far further back in time than its 18th century demeanour would have visitors believe. It is, in fact, a medieval borough or 'burh'. According to *English Medieval Boroughs – a handlist* by Maurice Berisford and H. P. R. Finberg, Wallingford was first mentioned in a Saxon land grant – as a port – in the year 945. It also has the distinction of a long account in Domesday Book and its castle (the ruins of which are now open to the public) was used as Henry and Matilda's stronghold during the civil war which ended in 1154.

The late 19th century drinking fountain in Wallingford Market Place.

It is worth looking at the bridge over the Thames close by the remains of the castle. Although it was largely rebuilt at the start of the 19th century, parts are medieval and it was certainly in existence at the time of the civil war. The town shows evidence of building in other periods, too, with some fine gabled and timber-framed houses from the 16th and 17th centuries.

The bridge across the Thames at Wallingford dates from medieval times.

8 Mongewell Park to Watlington

via Nuffield and Swyncombe Manor
9½ miles (15.1 km)

This section of the Ridgeway takes you along Grim's Ditch **48** and up into the Chiltern Hills, past Nuffield Common before descending through the scarp valleys to the little town of Watlington, half a mile away from the path.

If you are joining the Ridgeway from Wallingford, retrace your steps along the riverside footpath, turn left at **A** and go through the woods of Mongewell Park. Climb over a stile out of the woods, over another stile as indicated by a public footpath sign and into a line of trees again. In spring look for violets coming into bloom in small, isolated clumps. Wrens may fly low over the ground, and chiffchaffs sing their repetitive but welcome song. As you approach the road, the grassy track through the trees climbs a little. Go over another stile and out of the trees, turn right on to the road and cross it, taking care as the traffic is very fast. Pass through a wooden gate and ascend past Lark Rise on to the line of Grim's Ditch **48**.

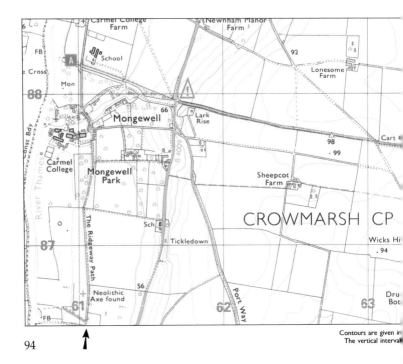

Contours are given in
The vertical interval

Continue to follow the path, walking on top of the bank. The remains of Grim's Ditch are hardly impressive in height though its length leads one to believe that its construction must have been a major undertaking, even if no one knows what its exact purpose was (see page 100).

Because of the denseness of the shrubbery on either side of the track here, which is a bridleway, only occasional glimpses of the surrounding countryside can be caught, but after the minor road from Crowmarsh Gifford at Cart Gap more of the landscape can be seen.

From Cart Gap, the path descends gently to another minor road which follows the line of the old Icknield Way, then the footpath takes you slowly uphill towards Oaken Copse, a marvellous place for bluebells in May. The path of the Ridgeway through the copse is clear enough, and then it descends again before the climb up Bachelor's Hill. Look out for more violets along the way.

From Bachelor's Hill, the bank and ditch are in evidence again and, in places, flints break through the surface of the path. You walk through a mixture of trees and open fields, up and down hill, past a white house and across stiles and various farm tracks, until you reach a T-junction. Here you go left (north) and

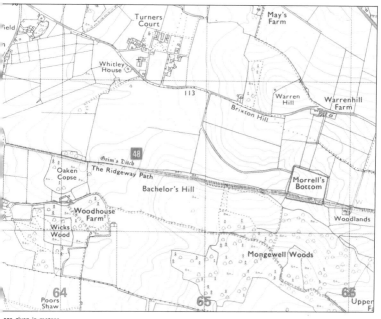

are given in metres
tical interval is 5m

ascend on a winding track, across a polegate, and on past The White House into the hamlet of Nuffield.

Turn right on to the road; in a stand of tall trees almost opposite there is a rookery. Pass Nuffield parish church **49** on the right; here there is a friendly sign to Ridgeway walkers, offering them water and shelter. May this sign long remain; thank you, Rector! Here you are 700 feet (212 metres) above sea level, the highest point in the southern Chilterns. Consequently, this place was of great importance long before there was a church here. The simple stone font, with its wooden cover, may be Saxon. It is thought that the four walls of the nave were built as long ago as A D 634, although the bulk of the church is about 900 years old.

Look for the Ridgeway sign opposite the church and head off to the east across a stile, soon reaching the Nuffield Common Golf Course clubhouse **50**. Your way across this busy course is marked by numbered white posts with the acorn symbol, each of which can be seen from its neighbour. After crossing two fairways (look carefully first), you go into some trees and the path takes you past Fairway Cottage, seemingly through the front garden, and comes out on to the A 423 road which leads to Nettlebed and Wallingford. There is parking for a few cars, a telephone box and bus stop, as well as the Crown public house with its quiet but friendly welcome.

From the Crown, continue down the grass steps and cross the road diagonally to the left, taking great care as visibility is poor and the traffic fast. Enter the small woodland through a five-bar gate, aiming to the north-west. After leaving the wood, the path crosses open fields. White posts indicate the way across them, then you go through a narrow strip of woodland guided by acorns. Turn right out of the trees and, once more, aim for the white post across the fields, obviously in an uphill direction. Continue in roughly the same direction between lines of thorn trees until you meet a rutted farm track. Turn right past Ewelme Park **51**, an impressive mock-Elizabethan house with its neatly mown lawns and rather incongruous, modern-looking windows. Shortly after passing the house, go straight over the crossing track and through the farmyard.

Aim for the Plantation where you bear left to the north. This is rich, open farmland punctuated by a number of plantations. Follow the headland path to the strangely named wood of Jacob's Tent, where the path descends quite steeply through delightful, open woodland. Fortunately, waymarking here

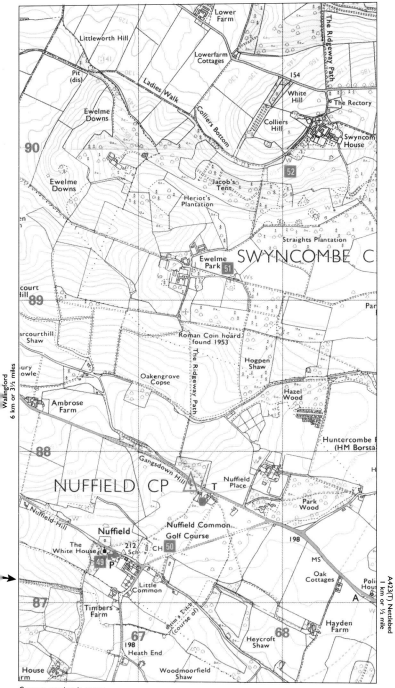

Contours are given in metres
The vertical interval is 5m

97

makes navigation very straightforward and this part of the walk passes, at first, through lovely, memorable countryside. At the end of the woods, cross a stile and descend across a field. For me, this area of Swyncombe House **52** is one of the most delightful interludes of the whole of the Ridgeway walk. Here we are, for a brief moment, walking among the epitome of rolling, rich, soft, green, typically English landscape which creates the impression that it has scarcely changed for generations.

On reaching the lane, Ladies Walk, turn right, heading more east of north for a while. After about 440 yards you pass through a gate. To the right is Swyncombe House. Swyncombe Manor was held by the Abbey of Bec in Normandy between 1086 and 1460. The bridleway takes you round to the right, past the beautifully restored little Church of St Botolph's, dating back to the 11th century with 13th and 14th century bells.

Just past the church, the lane bears to the left and shortly emerges on to a quiet minor road which crosses from east to west. The Ridgeway is now aiming just about due north, across the road and a stile. The hard, chalky path along the left-hand edge of a large field now descends quite steeply ahead into another valley before rising again, just as steeply, to enter a pleasant mixed wood with the bulk of the trees on the left at first. Continue along a slightly winding path through the woodland until the track bears a little to the north-east and the trees begin to thin out on the left. From here there are views to the north-west with Britwell Salome House just visible in the distance.

At the end of Dean Wood, most of which is to the right of the path, the Ridgeway bears to the north-west, becoming a rough farm track as it does so. In a further 880 yards the track turns sharply to the right just after passing the buildings of North Farm on the left. You are now on the Icknield Way **53**, which you first crossed part-way along Grim's Ditch (the Swan's Way rejoins from the left). After about 440 yards cross the minor road leading from Britwell Salome and continue in a north-easterly direction, eventually reaching Lys Farm House where the path continues in the same direction but, this time, as a metalled road. Cross Howe Road (the B480) near Icknield House and continue along the track with Watlington Hill to the north-east. Keep on until you reach the crossing with Hill Road which leads down into the small town of Watlington **54** and to a pleasant camp site at White Mark Farm.

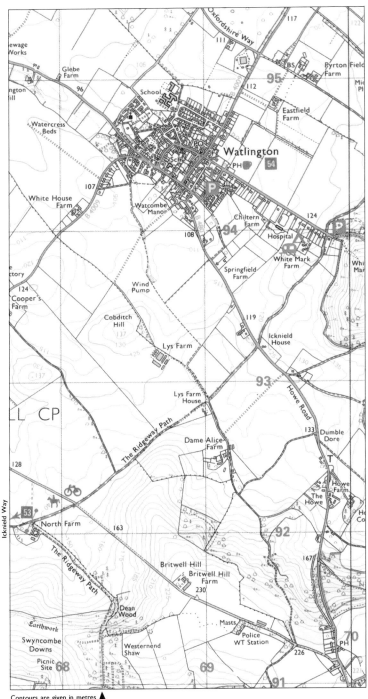

Contours are given in metres
The vertical interval is 5m

99

Trees overshadow the path along Grim's Ditch, an ancient earthwork with a possible defensive significance.

Grim's Ditch

Grim is another name for the Nordic god Odin, and 'Grim's Ditch' **48** was often used by the Saxons to name any existing earthwork they came across because they believed that, if they did not know who made the structure, then Odin or Wodin must have been responsible. No one knows for sure who built these earthworks, nor for what purpose, but it is possible that they may have had the same strategic importance as the Ridgeway hill forts, to defend the territory of the Romano-British inhabitants from invasion from the north.

It has also been suggested that the ditch may have separated two Iron Age estates, perhaps to keep the sheep in the north apart from pigs and cattle in the south. Even so, if the two peoples with their different farming practices were hostile, the ditch may still have had some defensive significance; it seems too major a work merely to contain stock and, at the least, may have made rustling more difficult.

Ewelme

The straggling village of Ewelme, nestling in the Chiltern foothills, is only 2½ miles (4 km) from either Ewelme Park or Swyncombe House, and is well worth a visit. It is best known for its splendid group of 15th century buildings – church, school and almshouses – and for its associations with Chaucer's granddaughter, Alice, Duchess of Suffolk (look out for 'Dame Alice Farm' further along the Ridgeway national trail near Watlington).

The Perpendicular church of St Mary the Virgin is high on the hill above the village. It is well preserved – the local Parliamentary commander protected it from destruction during the Civil War – and has interesting furnishings, brasses and two magnificent tombs: that of Duchess Alice herself, as well as the tomb of her father, Thomas Chaucer. It is also where Jerome K. Jerome, author of *Three Men in a Boat*, is buried. The almshouses, founded in 1437 by the Suffolks, are built around a small courtyard at the west end of the church, and are still in use today.

The name Ewelme is derived from 'lawelme' – a spring source – and even today the spring feeds the cress-filled chalk stream running beside the main street through the village. Pleasant cottages and a quiet location help to make Ewelme one of the prettiest villages in the Chilterns.

The 15th century almshouses at Ewelme, which enclose a small courtyard.

9 Watlington to Princes Risborough

past Lewknor and Chinnor
11 miles (17.5 km)

Much of the Ridgeway in this stretch is on the Upper Icknield Way (see page 110), which followed the lower chalk shelf at the foot of the north-western scarp of the Chilterns. The route is all on bridleways or country lanes, so this is a section that is suitable for horseriders or cyclists.

If you have stayed in Watlington **54**, walk back up Hill Road and turn left, below Watlington Hill, on to the Ridgeway, which runs along a gravelled lane that soon becomes a chalky and muddy track.

The lower parts of the hills are wood-cladded and, to the left, the flat farmland stretches out across the Oxfordshire plain. In some hawthorn bushes to my left, I had marsh tits for company on my April walk. After about 550 yards the track plunges between lines of trees, becoming muddy and deeply rutted, although the soil here is less obviously chalky. And in another 500 yards it crosses the partially metalled lane which is the Oxfordshire Way, a 65-mile (105-km) recreational route from Bourton-on-the-Water in the Cotswolds to Henley-on-Thames.

The lane winds uphill through the trees and is obviously used by horseriders. The shallow bank on the right-hand side of the lane was pockmarked with what could have been rabbit burrows although, at the entrance to one, there were the remains of a bird, which might have been the leftovers from a fox's meal, suggesting a change of ownership for at least one of the holes. I heard chiffchaffs and the occasional pheasant, and saw robins, finches, dunnock, tits and wrens. A rabbit, scutt showing white, dashed across the lane in front of me. There were clusters of white and purple violets at the edges of the track.

Slowly the Ridgeway begins to ascend with the steep, tree-clad, tumulus-like mound of Shirburn Hill to the right. In the distance, there is a barely audible hum which gradually increases. A glance at the map shows that the M 40 motorway is at least $1\frac{1}{2}$ miles (2.5 km) away but, even at this distance, it makes its noisy presence felt. The green lane continues to be fringed with ancient beeches, younger willows and occasional elms and yews, as well as dead trees. Emerging from the lane,

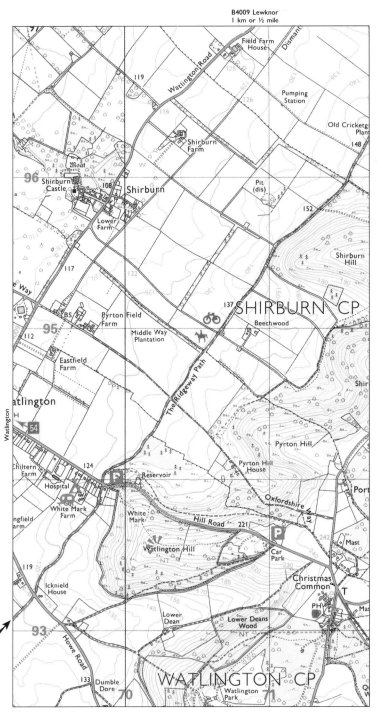

Shirburn
Field Farm House
Watlington Road
119
Pumping Station
Old Cricketg Plan
Shirburn Farm
148
Moat
96 Shirburn Castle
108
Shirburn
Pit (dis)
152
Lower Farm
Shirburn Hill
117
122
e Way
137 SHIRBURN CP
BS
Pyrton Field Farm
Beechwood
95
Middle Way Plantation
112
Shir
Eastfield Farm
The Ridgeway Path
atlington
Watlington
H
54
Pyrton Hill
Chiltern Farm
124
Pyrton Hill House
Reservoir
Port
Hospital
White Mark Farm
Oxfordshire
ngfield arm
White Mark
Hill Road
221
P
Watlington Hill
Car Park
Mast
NT
119
Christmas Common
T
Icknield House
93
Lower Dean
Lower Deans Wood
PH
Mas
Howe Road
NT
133 Dumble Dore
70
WATLINGTON CP
71
Watlington Park
Q

Contours are given in metres
The vertical interval is 5m

103

the track becomes broad and grassy once more, rising slowly uphill towards the motorway, which is now clearly visible on the immediate horizon directly ahead, as well as cutting a broad, grey swathe across the countryside to the left. To the right rises Bald Hill where there is part of a national nature reserve and, beyond the motorway, Beacon Hill, with the other part of the reserve. As the traffic roar grew louder, I realised why the siting of this road caused such controversy – in this case, the planners had their way and the national nature reserve of Aston Rowant **55** was cut in two.

Just before reaching the M 40, the Ridgeway crosses a metalled road running between Hill Farm and Lewknor, a little less than half a mile (1 km) to the north-west. On the other side of the tunnel under the M 40, the track is broad and badly scored by ruts in places but, by walking on the grassy verges or on the ridge in the middle, the going can be quite comfortable. Leaving the noise of the motorway behind, Beacon Hill rises up to the right. Now the track follows a tree-lined bank. The National Nature Reserve of Aston Rowant, part owned, part leased, and part held by agreement, occupies 315 acres (126 hectares) and includes chalk grassland with several kinds of orchid, and scrub on the slopes where juniper, privet and yew grow in abundance. There is beech woodland, too, with ash, wild cherry and oak. Further information about the reserve can be obtained from the Nature Conservancy Council's regional office at Foxhold House, Crookham Common, Newbury, or from the Warden at 1 Field Farm Cottages, Menmarsh Road, Worminghall, Aylesbury, Bucks.

The A 40 road, which you cross next, can be busy. The brick and flint house here, Beacon Cottage Country Guest House, helpfully hangs a dustbin bag on its boundary fence along the Ridgeway.

The tree-root-bound rough track continues straight ahead with primroses brightening the way in spring. The tree-covered ridge of Aston Hill is to the right and, again, the going could be very muddy in wet weather. In April, the fields to the right may be sown with perfectly uniform green grass and oilseed rape. Ahead and to the right, the wooded slopes of Kingston Hill rise to its trig point at 678 feet (206 metres). By any standards, it can be rough underfoot; when the track is wet, it is deeply rutted by farm vehicles and, when dry, although a horse could get through, I suspect even a mountain bike would have some problems. You now cross a bridleway which leads to Aston

Rowant to the north and Aston Hill to the south. In this area, for the first time along the Ridgeway, I saw the charming little long-tailed tits flitting among the trees. Ahead, and a little to the right, the white marker posts of a rarely-used point-to-point racecourse come into view. The going becomes a little easier again here, although it can still be wet, muddy and rutted in parts. Cross a track leading to Grove Farm and the way becomes grassy again.

Soon you cross the minor road which leads to Kingston Blount **56** in the north. The route continues straight ahead as a

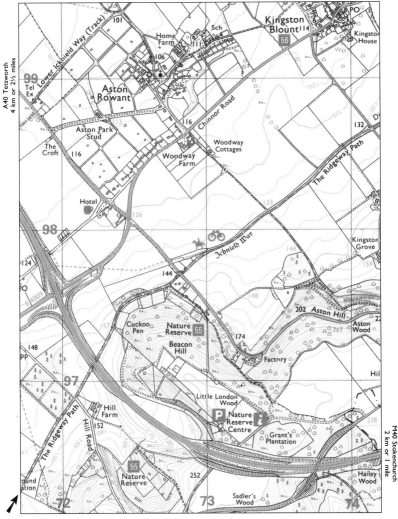

Contours are given in metres
The vertical interval is 5m

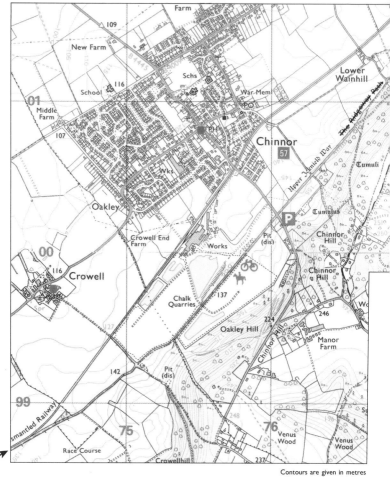

Contours are given in metres
The vertical interval is 5m

broad, grassy, hedge-lined track. Ahead and a little to the left rise the twin chimneys of the Chinnor cement works, one of which issues a plume of water vapour. And immediately to the left of the path, the line of a railway, which is in use only from the cement works eastwards, is picked out by its hedges. Beside the cement works are water-filled quarry pits, one of which has been made into a nature reserve attracting Canada geese. The path ascends with Oakley Hill to the right before dropping down to the road from Crowell Hill to Chinnor **57**, half a mile away.

Across the road the track is creamy white and chalky once again, and climbs steadily along the lower slopes of Bledlow Ridge **58**, on the edge of the woods. Look out for dog's mercury and primroses. At Wain Hill Cottage, turn right by a red-brick

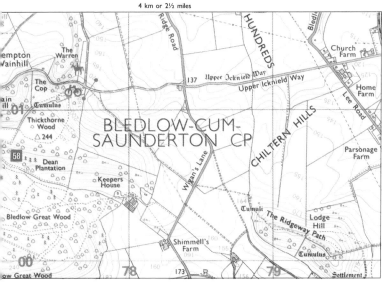

rs are given in metres
ertical interval is 5m

house, and once again you seem to be intruding into a garden but the wooden signposts are reassuring. You are now walking eastwards and have crossed into Buckinghamshire.

With the scarp of the Bledlow Ridge rising steeply ahead and to the right, this is an attractive spot. Once again the trail begins gently to rise as a broad, muddy lane on the edge of the wood. Emerging from the trees, and travelling a little to the south of east, tracks lead off to left and right. Continue onwards to where you see the wooden Ridgeway signpost, at which point you leave the Icknield Way, cross a stile to the right, and go into a field which you cross diagonally. On the far, upward slope of the field to the right of some trees, the path can be seen working its way up across the hill in a direction a little south of east. At the top of the slope, the rise of Lodge Hill can be seen.

The path stays close to the fence, goes across a stile and carries on down with the fence on your right to the Bledlow road, where you climb over a high, awkward stile and cross the road diagonally to the left to another stile. The path is then quite obvious across the field. Cross another stile and the broad path across the next field is clearly defined forking to the left. Lodge Hill seems to grow ever closer. You are now heading towards a line of coppiced trees. Go over the stile or pass through the gap in the trees and turn right. Follow the path along the edge of the field with the trees on your right until the boundary of the field turns sharply left. The Ridgeway route continues ahead and upwards on to the slopes of Lodge Hill.

As it rises to the summit of the hill the path becomes quite steep. This is soft, rabbit-grazed turf with small hazel trees and wild roses. On the long, high ridge, the views to both sides are splendid. Continue across the hill towards a line of trees before descending. In fact, you must bear a little left down the hill towards a stile. Do not wander right, into a danger area where there may be shooting. Lodge Hill would make a lovely spot for a summer picnic.

Continue downhill towards a gap in a hedge which meets the one you are following. Go through the gap, and follow the acorn and blue arrow to the right of a well-clipped hawthorn hedge. Follow the hedge downhill and, 100 yards before the electricity pylons, turn left. Follow the path, keeping the hedge on your right, as it winds down towards the minor road which leads to Saunderton, about $1\frac{1}{4}$ miles (2 km) to the north. From here it is possible to see Lacey Green **59** on the hillside ahead with its restored smock mill, one of the oldest in Britain.

Cross the road on to the gravel drive – which is a footpath – that leads to a single red-brick house. Go to the right of the house and then across the broad field ahead towards a line of trees. At a double stile, turn right and follow a hedge before turning left at an acorn-marked post and following a line of old hawthorn trees.

With the railway ahead, go down the slope to yet another stile and follow the fence. Cross the railway line with care by a white fence and go into a thicket. Go through two kissing gates, over the top of the railway tunnel to a third kissing gate.

At this gate go straight across the field, which may be planted with crops. Pass directly between two pylons towards two converging hedgerows. The path emerges on to a minor road – the Upper Icknield Way again. (If walking east to west, you need to cross the field at approximately 45°, making for the kissing gate.) Follow the road to the right, and descend to cross Shootacre Lane. On the hillside ahead, you can make out the outline of Whiteleaf Cross carved into the slope, although from here it looks like a white horse. Continue along the road to the A 4010 High Wycombe–Princes Risborough road, and turn left towards Princes Risborough **60**. There is a pavement along the right-hand side of the road and, after the quiet of the hills, the traffic noise seems wearing. Just after Culverton Lane, about half a mile on, there is a public footpath to the right which, although it is not the official route, does rejoin it and cut off a corner, provided you do not mind negotiating two more stiles.

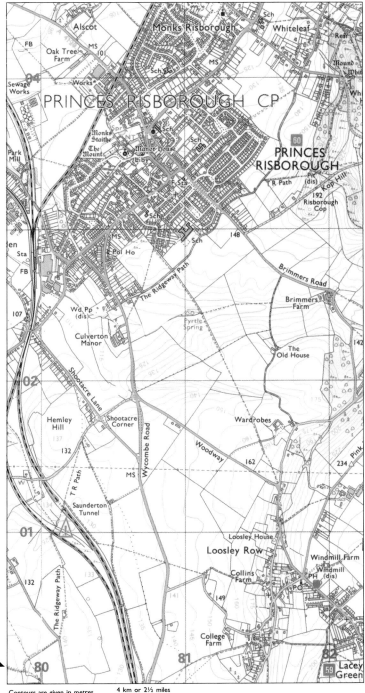

Alscot

Monks Risborough

Whiteleaf

FB

Oak Tree Farm

MS
101

Sch

MS

94

Sewage Works

Works

PRINCES RISBOROUGH CP

Monks Staithe

The Mount

Sch

Manor House

Sch

PRINCES RISBOROUGH

Park Mill

F Sta

T R Path

Pit (dis)

Kop Hill

192
Risborough Cop

Sch

MS

148

en

Sta

Pol Ho

Sch

FB

The Ridgeway Path

Brimmers Road

Brimmers Farm

107

Wd Pp (dis)

Pyrtle Spring

Culverton Manor

The Old House

142

102

Shootacre Lane

Hemley Hill

Shootacre Corner

Wardrobes

Pink

137

132

Wycombe Road

Woodway

162

234

T R Path

MS

Saunderton Tunnel

01

Loosley House

Loosley Row

Windmill Farm

Windmill PH (dis)

132

The Ridgeway Path

Collins Farm

PO

149

141

College Farm

80

81

82

Lacey Green

59

Contours are given in metres
The vertical interval is 5m

4 km or 2½ miles
A4010 Bradenham

109

The Upper Icknield Way near Princes Risborough.

The official route, as signposted, turns right off the Wycombe Road in about another 100 yards into a cul-de-sac lane called the Upper Icknield Way. The Ridgeway goes north-eastwards, staying on the southern outskirts of the town. You soon pass the point where the short cut mentioned earlier rejoins the route and, a little beyond that, another footpath crosses the way. Soon you pass a school on the left and then some small bungalows, and descend to Brimmers Road. Turn left and walk down to Princes Risborough if you are planning to stop here.

The Icknield Way

The Icknield Way was a trading route from Norfolk to the south-west, which has now largely been absorbed into the present network of roads. Look carefully on the maps; you can follow much of the line of the Icknield Way from the Thames (Streatley was thought to be a major ford) to Ivinghoe, on B roads and tracks, along both the Upper and Lower Ways.

There are many theories as to its history, but it is not as old as the Ridgeway. The name 'Icknield' may derive from the Iceni, who could have used it as a warpath, or from old British words for 'upper'. The fact is that its precise origins are lost in the mists of time. What *is* sure is that it followed ridges, where possible, and the lower chalk shelf, which offered a better route than the 'clay-with-flints' and the thick woodland of the Chilterns. This is the line followed by the Upper Icknield Way; the Lower Way is on the clay and may have been a later, possibly Roman, route.

From Ivinghoe the Icknield Way goes on to Thetford, where it connects with the Peddars Way. The route of the Icknield Way from Streatley to the west is via Blewbury and Wantage to Wanborough, following a line to the north of the Ridgeway. One of the best books on the Icknield Way is Edward Thomas's account of his walk along the way before the First World War; even today much of the landscape he admired is still there to be enjoyed.

10 Princes Risborough to Wendover

past Whiteleaf Cross and Chequers
6 miles (9.5 km)

From Princes Risborough **60**, walk up Brimmers Road to rejoin the Ridgeway on the left, where it follows the Upper Icknield Way. Walk past the backs of houses, then by some playing fields. At a fork in the ways, go to the right, uphill towards Risborough Cop and Kop Hill. You go past a line of thorn trees on the left towards the woodland, where you can see a stile with a white acorn on it. Cross this stile and bear left into the woodland where the track becomes stepped. It is steep going here. Before reaching the top of the hill, cross another stile and go more or less straight ahead. Continue uphill, keeping Risborough Cop on the right and, eventually, you reach a minor road leading from Brimmers Road. From here walk diagonally across the field as indicated by an acorn on a tree trunk. Another, more obvious acorn is on the fence post towards the edge of a wood. Climb over a stile and enter the wood, following marker posts. You come on to a partially metalled but narrow track. Pass between concrete gateposts and out on to the road. Cross the road, maintaining your direction, and then turn left into the car park for Whiteleaf Cross, as indicated by green signposts.

From the signpost pointing to Whiteleaf Cross **61** there is a confusion of paths, but white acorns indicate the Ridgeway (which is now a bridleway) through the woodland across the edge of Whiteleaf Hill. You emerge on to the grassy clearing with splendid views ahead to the north. On the slope of the hill, however, is the Whiteleaf Cross. It is the earliest of the Chiltern hill figures. First documented in 1742, the cross may have been carved by monks in the 15th or 16th centuries for devotional or perhaps navigational purposes.

You turn right into the heart of Giles Wood, following the path slightly north of east, and then bear due north again towards Lower Cadsden. Behind you is the tree-clad hollow of The Hangings. The way then descends sharply to the Cadsdean Road – this can be very slippery in wet weather. On either side of the track the hill plunges away as you walk through the beech woodland. Towards the foot of the hill, go across a stile or through the metal gate. There is parking here only for the patrons of The Plough public house.

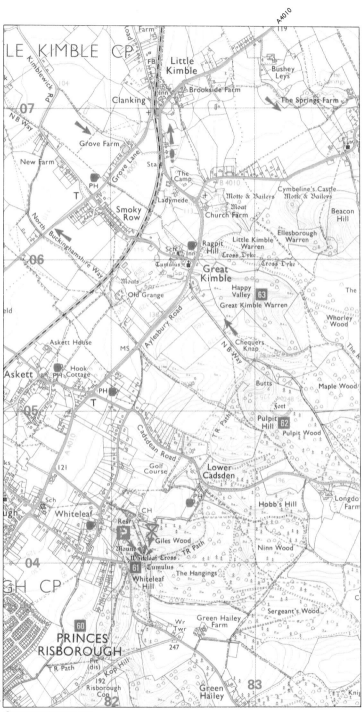

Contours are given in metres
The vertical interval is 5m

113

Continue past the pub on the left. As you emerge on to the Cadsdean Road, there are two possible routes. The definitive (i.e. 'official') path involves a walk of about 200 yards down the road to the left and then a steep climb northwards between fences about 3 feet (1 metre) apart. A far better alternative route involves crossing the Cadsdean Road diagonally towards a post saying 'No horses' and beyond that, painted on a tree trunk, a white acorn and yellow arrow pointing the way slightly east of north. (This is currently a permissive route.)

Go into the coppiced woodland heading towards the rise of Pulpit Hill 62. This nature reserve of Grangelands and Pulpit Hill is owned by Bucks County Council and the National Trust but the local naturalists' trust, BBONT, manages it. Here, though, the downland turf has been worn away to the detriment of the landscape and animal life. Riders should use only the marked track and not gallop.

Follow the waymarks across the nature reserve until you come to a crossing bridleway.* At this point the official path joins from the left. Go straight over and continue uphill. With the wooded heights of Pulpit Hill to the right, continue north-eastwards across its lower ridge. Pass the Butts on your right and go into woodland over a stile, climbing steps to emerge into a deep cutting (meeting the North Bucks Way). Turn right and, a little way up the gully, go over the stile on the left. The tumulus on the small hill on your left is Chequers Knap.

(*Westbound travellers should look out for the start of the alternative route at the crossing bridleway. The official route goes to the right, and after a few yards turns left through a thicket and straight across an arable field to the top of the steep bank, which the path descends to the Cadsdean Road. The alternative route goes straight over the bridleway, across the Grangelands reserve to the Cadsdean Road, emerging almost opposite the road to 'The Plough'.)

Now head slightly north of east across the valley. Route-finding is not immediately obvious but there is a fairly well-trodden path and, on the other side of the cutting, there is what looks like a stile for which to aim. This is curious, undulating, gullied country. In the valley, the footpath takes you on to an obvious track and the route bears to the right. For westward travellers, the way is to some extent more obvious.

The footpath now runs for some distance above a deep valley to the left. This is delightful walking country – it is called Great Kimble Warren and Happy Valley 63.

Grangelands and Pulpit Hill, now a nature reserve known for its chalk grassland flora.

Climb over another stile and cross the open, grassy field where the path is quite well worn. Aim for the gates and stile on the other side. The path now veers to the south, skirting the north-eastern side of Maple Wood to avoid entering the actual grounds of Chequers **64**, the Prime Minister's country residence. This is pleasant, open farmland with the 16th century house of Chequers partly visible behind some trees as you cross a stile and walk by the edge of the wood. At the end of Maple Wood, you are directed across the farmland to the left, over two more stiles, and on to the drive of Chequers itself. This house was given as a country home for the Prime Minister in 1917 by Lord Lee of Fareham. Thoughtfully, what could have been muddy patches by the stiles have been bricked in. Cross the gravel drive and head for another stile in the fields opposite. Climb over the stile, cross the road, and follow the broad track into the trees to the left of a group of white houses.

Proceed uphill into the woods following the acorn symbols. This is a fine beech wood. On reaching the shoulder of the hill, two acorns tell you to turn left and, after about 20 yards, turn right again and into the heart of the wood. Here you must just keep your eyes open to follow the acorns for there is no very obvious path. In parts, however, the way is deeply rutted by horses' hoofs and very muddy. In May, bluebells carpet the woodland floor. Compass users should head roughly northwards. Turn left on to a gated farm road and then right on to a minor road heading gently uphill. Almost opposite a red-brick house, a signpost and acorns tell you to cross the road and enter the woodland on Lodge Hill. Once again, follow the acorns through the wood. Climb a stiled fence, where there is also a helpful dog gate. Turn left towards the edge of the hill. To the left, there are lovely views towards Beacon Hill, and down into the village of Ellesborough, with the church and Ellesborough Manor clearly visible across the golf course.

Once again, you are on a broad swathe of the rabbit-cropped grass which makes comfortable walking. By the trig point at 845 feet (257 metres) atop Coombe Hill **65** there is a grand-looking monument capped with a golden fluted ball. The views in all directions are spectacular so, perhaps not surprisingly, this land is in the ownership of the National Trust. The Ridgeway does not actually go to the monument itself but the short diversion is worth a little effort just for the breathtaking views.

From the monument, simply head just north of eastwards again until you pick up the Ridgeway. The path is obvious and skirts along the edge of the hill – in places it is even paved with brick. Arriving at the wood and the corner of some fencing, the main path bears to the right with the fence to the left. Here you should turn left and, as you descend the upper slopes of the hill, an acorn painted on a tree to the right of the reverse side of a National Trust sign shows your way back on to the route. Pass through a kissing gate and into a gully. There is a well-defined and waymarked path. Ahead and to the left, the large village of Wendover comes into view and, as you enter the wood, the path descends gradually across Bacombe Hill **66**. Just before what looks like the end of the Bacombe Hill ridge, the path forks to the left down the hill as a broadly defined path on a bank. Even though the road and Wendover are so close, this is pleasant walking, with only the occasional dog walker to greet

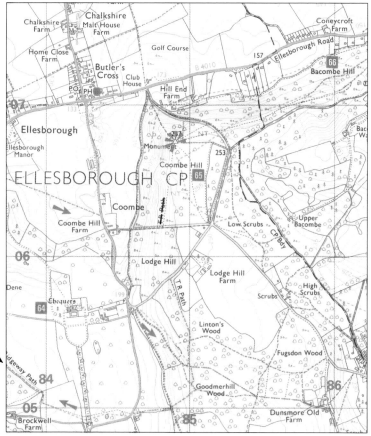

Contours are given in metres
The vertical interval is 5m

you. Here, the steepening gradient is eased by broad steps cut into the path. Bacombe Hill is owned and maintained by Buckinghamshire County Council.

On reaching the B4010, where there is parking for perhaps two cars, turn right and take the road down into Wendover **67**. Cross the railway line via the road bridge where Wendover station is signposted to the left. At a mini-roundabout, continue straight ahead towards Aylesbury and Tring. It is now sensible to walk on the right-hand side of the road because you will shortly be turning right when leaving Wendover.

The Chiltern beechwoods

Anyone travelling the eastern 'half' of the Ridgeway cannot fail to notice two important natural and not-quite-so-natural features of the landscape – the chalk escarpment and plateau which comprise the Chiltern Hills and the extensive beech-woods which shade much of that ridge. Deposited in warm Upper Cretaceous seas some 80 million years ago, the major structures of the chalk rock of south-east England, such as the Chiltern Hills, were formed during the same great heavings of the planet that threw up the Alpine mountain chain about 50 million years later. But it was not until the extensive oakwoods, which once clothed much of England, began to be cleared in Neolithic times that the beech could predominate, even though it is a native English tree. In strict ecological terms, then, beechwoods are not natural, but that hardly matters to passers-through – they seem natural enough now although, in places, evidence of coppicing does suggest that they have at least been managed. Indeed, they continue to be so in some areas.

The nature of beechwoods is quite different from that of other deciduous woodland, and this becomes obvious as you pass between the tall, smooth, pewter-grey trunks and beneath the dense canopy of light-green leaves up to 100 feet (30 metres) above your head. Even in the brightest days of summer, only a leaf-filtered twilight penetrates to the woodland floor littered with mast and the crisp brown leaves of earlier summers. Apart from the harsh notes of chiffchaffs, the descending, musical trill of willow warblers from high overhead, or the alarm call of a disturbed blackbird, beechwoods are often eerily quiet.

The soils on the Chilterns may vary from deep, rich loams to shallow, acidic types on the clay-with-flints which caps the chalk in places, or, where it does not, thin chalky soil predominates. There are beechwoods to be found on all these

Contours are given in metres
The vertical interval is 5m

6 km or 3½ miles
A413 Great Missenden

soils, although the trees may grow taller where the substrate is richer and deeper. It is the peculiarly shallow and very wide-reaching root system of the beech which enables it to flourish where other trees cannot. And, once it has become established, a beechwood's dense canopy of leaves high above restricts the light so much that few other plants can survive in the darker parts. Thus, in many places, the only other bushes or shrubs to be seen are occasional hollies or yews, although brambles may straggle across quite large areas. At ground level, dog's mercury or sanicle may grow, bird's-nest orchids may throw up their rusty brown flower spikes, often unseen, where the soil is rich in humus from the decaying leaves and lime from the chalk, and, in autumn, there is a variety of fungi associated with the beech trees. Rarely do plants carpet the beechwood floor as they may do in other woodland types.

It is probably safe to say that all of today's Chiltern beech trees have been planted. From about the 17th century, beech wood has had a commercial worth, initially to supply a cheap source of fuel and charcoal for London and then, particularly in the 18th century, for furniture-making, with an industry centred on High Wycombe. In today's slang, 'bodger' is a word often applied to someone who turns out poor-quality work, especially carpentry or DIY. In the 1700s, however, and even in its strictly correct meaning now, a bodger was a craftsman skilled at turning and carving wood, especially beech, to make chairs, and individual bodgers flourished throughout the Chiltern woods. It is likely that the modern slang usage has evolved through an alteration of the word 'botcher' and because a bodger was someone associated with working in wood.

There are few bodgers left today but beechwood is still used for furniture-making, and the Chiltern beechwoods continue to have commercial and leisure-time value.

A CIRCULAR WALK ON THE RIDGEWAY AND NORTH BUCKS WAY

6 miles (10 km) (see maps on pages 113 and 117)
Parts of this walk are complicated to describe but a leaflet depicting the walk is available from Buckinghamshire County Council, County Engineers Department, County Hall, Aylesbury, Bucks. The easiest starting point is the railway station and car park to the south of Little Kimble (see map on page 113). From here, walk northwards into Little Kimble on the A4010 Aylesbury road. Then turn right on to a route leading to Ellesborough Manor. From here (see map on page 117), head south and then south-east towards Coombe Hill Farm. Turn right on to the minor road and, shortly afterwards, left then right, following the route marked on the map, eventually climbing up to join the Ridgeway Path. Follow the Ridgeway briefly south and then west, skirting Chequers **64**, until it joins with the North Bucks Way at Chequers Knap (page 113). Continue north-westwards until you reach the minor road near New Farm. Turn left on to the road but where the North Bucks Way forks off left, continue on the road turning right. Where the road takes a sharp turn to the left, turn right on to a path leading to the B4009 Grove Lane. Turn left, go under the railway, and turn immediately right and back to the station and car park.

Woods are an important part of the Chilterns landscape, but they do need to be managed.

121

11 Wendover to Wigginton

through Barn Wood and Pavis Wood
6 miles (9.8 km)

A feature of this stretch of the path is the woodlands, some of which are worth taking a side trip to visit; see page 126.

In Wendover **67**, go past the library, toilets and car park on the right. Just before you reach the clock tower and another mini-roundabout turn right towards St Mary's Church and into a narrow lane called Heron Path, as indicated by the Ridgeway signpost. As the path crosses a narrow lane, bear a little to the left and straight across the lane, as indicated by the acorn-marked telegraph post. On reaching Heron Cottage, a footpath crosses the stream to the left but you go right in front of the cottage. About 20 yards further on, the way is confirmed by a signpost and you cross another driveway and head upslope towards the church.

As you reach the road, turn left immediately in front of the church. The churchyard of St Mary the Virgin is well kept, with flowers gracing the flint walls. Follow the minor road past the church to a more major road, cross it and continue straight ahead into a 'no through road', passing to the left of a cream-painted house. You are now heading south-east on the metalled lane towards a line of wooded hills. Past some farm buildings the lane becomes a gravel and dirt track. Where it turns back into the farm buildings, carry on to a fork in the lane.

The way ascends towards a red-brick farmhouse with its barn behind – Boswells Farm. Atop the main house, there is a small bell and clock tower with a charming fox weather vane. Continue straight on past a curious little wooden cottage and into a band of woodland where blue periwinkles line the verges. Where the lane forks left, continue straight on towards the hill ahead.

Another 20 yards or so after taking a left-hand lane, turn left again through a couple of wooden gateposts. Bear left at yet another fork where there is a wire fence to the right and a small plantation of young conifers. In another 30 yards there is one more fork where, this time, you head right up the hill as indicated, into the open woodland and coppice of Barn Wood, with dog's mercury and occasional clumps of primroses in early spring. Continue up into the wood. When the trees are not in leaf, there are glimpses of the wooded hills and vales to the left.

Contours are given in metres
The vertical interval is 5m

As the slope eases, the track continues straight on upwards towards a clearing but a faded yellow arrow indicates that you turn left. The route here is not obvious, but continues to skirt around the edge of the hill; for compass users in a north-easterly direction. Every now and then there are odd hollows by the side of the path. The going here could be muddy especially in wet weather. Eventually the way becomes broad and grassy as you walk among the willow, hazel, hawthorn and beech trees. You are passing through the southern fringes of Wendover Woods, part of the Forestry Commission's Chiltern Forest (see page 126).

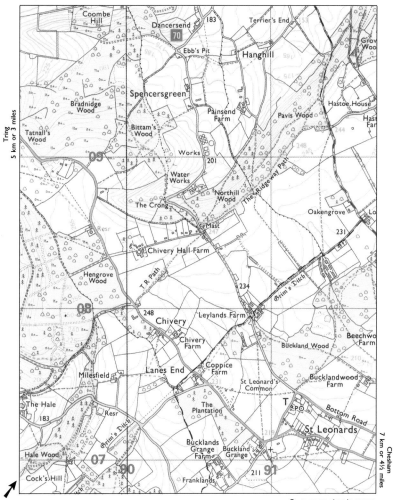

Contours are given in metres
The vertical interval is 5m

The track becomes broader, muddier and more rutted and occasionally there are paths crossing it. Shortly before Milesfield, pass through a gate and on to a road. Turn right on to the road and then immediately left across it by a house. Descend a little through the mature woodland. To the right is the broad, grassy green clearing of Milesfield itself while on the left is the deep, wooded vale of The Hale. At the bottom of the slope, turn right up a deep gully where you join a bridleway.

The slope eases, you pass a white-painted cottage on the right and emerge on to Aston Hill Road. Directly opposite, and

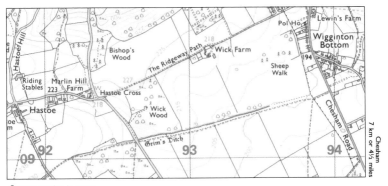

Contours are given in metres
The vertical interval is 5m

adjacent to a dormer-windowed bungalow, cross a waymarked stile through the hedge. After passing the corner of the hedge, aim for the radio mast ahead, keeping the hedge to the right. Just at the end of a small group of conifers, another stile takes you over a wooden fence, where you go diagonally across the field towards the mast and some farm buildings. The compass bearing is 44°. You cross the stile and arrive at the road to the right of the mast. Turn left down the road for a very short distance and then turn right into the wood as indicated. Follow the line of the woods, staying just inside their edge.

Emerging from Pavis Wood, cross a stile and take the road almost opposite, which leads gently downhill towards Hastoe. Your way takes you straight across into Church Lane, as indicated by the Ridgeway sign, and then the curious school-like buildings of Marlin Hill Farm soon come into view. Shortly after this, you arrive at Hastoe Cross. Cross the road, pass through a gate, and go on to a farm track where Wick Wood soon comes into sight.

In about 880 yards you pass the buildings of Wick Farm and the going becomes a neat, hedge-lined, gravel drive. For those stopping in Wigginton, it is possible to carry on past the point where the Ridgeway goes to the left and on to a metalled road with houses on the left. It then joins another road with Wigginton Bottom to the right and Wigginton itself to the left. Another public right of way leads off the minor road into Wigginton **68**.

You could then walk to Tring through Bulls Wood and Tring Park, or take a bus to Tring or Chesham. Alternatively, Tring station is not far along the Ridgeway (see next chapter for directions).

Wendover Woods, where the Forestry Commission offers walks and picnic are

Woods in the area

You may want to take time to divert from the Ridgeway to explore one of the woods in this part of the Chilterns.

Wendover Woods **69**, owned by the Forestry Commission, cover 400 acres (160 hectares) and offer a variety of walks, picnic areas, a wayfaring course and trails for horseriders (for which a permit is required). As well as coniferous woods, there is mixed woodland at Aston Hill Coppice and beech hangers. Contact the Forestry Commission's Chilterns office for details: tel. Wendover (0296) 625825.

At the north-eastern end of Wendover Woods is the 70-acre (28-hectare) BBONT reserve, Dancer's End **70**, with its more typical Chiltern woodland. This reserve is best in spring and summer, when a rich variety of plant species can be seen.

On a much larger scale is the Ashridge Estate **71**, to the south-east of Ivinghoe Beacon. This 4,000-acre (1,600-hectare) National Trust property has been famous for its beeches and oaks since the 18th century and has many paths which lead through the woods and heaths. Access is via the B4506 between Ringshall and Berkhamsted, or from the Ridgeway via a number of footpaths and bridleways from Tring station onwards.

12 Wigginton to Ivinghoe Beacon

past Tring Station and Pitstone Hill
5½ miles (8.8 km)

At last, the final stretch of your journey along the Ridgeway. This part of the path takes you down from the Chilterns and on to the chalk grassland of the Ivinghoe Hills. Since the path passes by Tring station, it is a very accessible section of the Ridgeway.

Before reaching the end of the gravel drive and the road to Wigginton **68**, turn left over a stile as indicated by a Ridgeway signpost. You are now on a grassy footpath, with the backs of houses to the right and a fence and fields to the left, heading for Bull's Wood. Just before reaching the wood, turn sharp right and climb over a stile. Here there is a wooden Ridgeway sign and, at another, the path soon makes a left turn to follow the eastern boundary of Bull's Wood in a direction a little west of north. Cross a lane and there is now a laurel hedge on the right and another plantation on the left. Ignore any turnings into the wood. Quite a lot of this woodland has now been replanted with young trees interspersed with bushes of broom. Beside a brick house with mock Tudor chimneys there is a stile, and the Ridgeway turns to the right to take you out on to a minor road.

Cross the road and the stile opposite into a field. There are attractive views to the left across the plain and to the hills ahead. You are now travelling along a fence-lined path towards Langton Wood. You pass a trig point on the path. Somewhat surprisingly, for there is no real feeling of great elevation, you are at a height of 710 feet (216 metres). To the left, the roar of traffic on the downslope side is from the A41(M). Climb over stiles – a single and then a double – and go into the field where there is a fence and a wood on the left. Cross another stile, still keeping the barbed wire fence to the left, and skirt along the edge of the field. Cross a minor road and carry on down until you reach the A41 trunk road which follows the line of the Roman road, Akeman Street.

Cross the road and walk down the verge to the right as directed. At Pen Beech Lodge, look for the Ridgeway sign, a stile, and another sign saying 'Public Footpath Tring Station' (the rumble of trains may also indicate that the station is not far away). Cross the stile and follow the path. This might once have

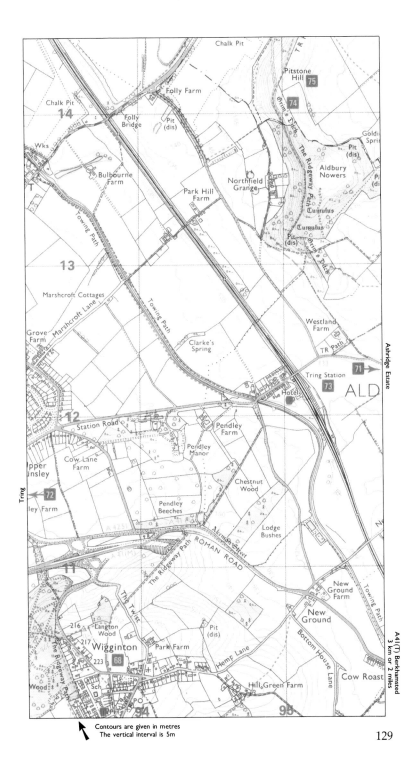

Contours are given in metres
The vertical interval is 5m

129

been a pleasant path with the beech hedge and the woodland to the left but it is now marred by a tall wire fence supported on strong wooden posts. Climb over another stile on to a gravel drive and you are still heading downslope. Do not be tempted to turn right here. Where the drive turns left into the wood continue onwards on the grassy path – there is no waymarking here but the direction is obvious.

There is a kissing gate on to a minor road. Turn left. In about 275 yards you will reach a T-junction. To the left is the main part of the town of Tring **72**, about $1\frac{1}{2}$ miles (2.5 km) along Station Road. Turn right, however, and cross the Grand Union Canal. In another 275 yards there is the Royal Hotel, offering cream teas and hotel and restaurant facilities as well as bars open to non-residents. There is a bus stop opposite. Shortly after this, there is Tring railway station **73** which, therefore, is some distance from the town centre. Cross the railway line and continue along the road past the minor road to the left. Continue along the main road, then turn left on to a metalled driveway which heads uphill and is clearly signposted. There is a wooden gate here. Continue straight on up a muddy track towards a wooden fence. Pass through another gate and turn sharp left. Continue gently uphill on the tree-lined path passing Westland Farm on the left. This is a bridleway which could be muddy in wet weather. Although it scarcely shows on the map you are following some quite old-looking woodland to the left of the track. At a crossing of paths, a Ridgeway signpost and an acorn tell you to fork right on to a broad track heading uphill and into some woodland. Where the track comes into a gully and bears to the right, there are waymarks showing the route to the left and up steps. The route undulates around the edge of the hill following the line of another Grim's Ditch **74**. It is pleasant walking through the wood; it continues to be waymarked and any rises are aided by the steps.

As I walked along in April, I was accompanied by the eerie yowling of peacocks, which I guessed must have been at Northfield Grange on the low ground to the west, and I was also aware of the presence of marsh tits. The way is now a broad, undulating dirt path through the woodland and cannot be mistaken. The route then begins to descend again across Pitstone Hill **75** and the cement works seems to fill the whole of the view ahead – a real blot on the landscape. If you are able to forget it, however, the patchwork of fields and buildings in the valley offers a more pleasing aspect.

A narrow boat on the Grand Union Canal, which stretches from London to Derbyshire.

Emerging from the woods, the way is clearly signposted along the edge of the hill where the earthworks of Grim's Ditch become more obvious. Below, milky blue waters have flooded the scar of a pit where chalk was extracted to feed the cement works. The narrow chalk track is easy to distinguish along the lip of the hill. Here it is best to stay on the uphill side of Grim's Ditch and the path is now just a grassy route to the left of a fence with the final destination, Ivinghoe Beacon **76**, clearly visible on the immediate horizon. Also visible is Pitstone windmill, one of the oldest postmills in the country. Owned by the National Trust, it is open on summer Sundays and bank holiday afternoons. Do not be tempted to stray down the hill following the line of the ditch and bank; the occasional waymark on a fencepost makes the route evident. The pits on the hillside are thought to be the remains of prehistoric flint mines; flints have been found in the area.

The descent from Pitstone Hill to the minor road between Ivinghoe and Aldbury takes you well to the right of the hill, then turns left on to the road and immediately right by some wooden posts. There is car parking space here. Now almost at the end of the journey, after all the ups and downs of the previous days, you remember that you are walking along a ridgeway. But there is one more valley to cross and one more ascent to make – the final one on to Ivinghoe Beacon itself.

The route ahead is obvious enough, into a shallow valley; follow it towards a triangle of trees across open farmland. Although Ivinghoe Beacon is not a particularly imposing hill, its isolation and position are good reasons why it should have been used as a beacon hill. Crossing the arable field on a hard, chalky white path you begin gently to ascend. Somehow the last few miles of any long-distance walk seem to be the longest and hardest. Perhaps this is the result of anticipating the end of one's efforts.

Having crossed the field, go over a stile and into sheep grazing land, then begin the ascent of Steps Hill, one of the Ivinghoe hills. Incombe Hole to the left is a deep curving gully carved into the hillside. Just as you reach the woodland, bear left and continue to rise steadily. Approaching the summit of Steps Hill, you can look back towards Grim's Ditch and see the path you have trodden. It looks a long way indeed and, although you cannot see it, you have journeyed 85 miles (137 km). This might be only a couple of hours by car but it is much longer on foot.

There is a sign here saying: WARNING. THIS LAND WAS FORMERLY USED FOR MILITARY TRAINING. DO NOT TOUCH ANY METAL OBJECTS LYING ABOUT. At the summit of Steps Hill, the track forks to the right through a gate by a stile. This is a permissive bridleway maintained by the National Trust. The official route, however, goes to the left of the stile and strikes north-west across a field to the edge of scrub. As you emerge from the thicket, you can see the descent and then the ascent of the Beacon with its trig point on the top. Follow the waymarks to a stile and continue across open ground to the road.

Cross the road with care before the final, undulating climb up a broad farm track. After about 33 yards, turn left towards the Beacon. The final ascent is on a steep, chalky, rutted path which could be very slippery when it is wet. From the top of the Beacon, reached breathless but satisfied, there are superb views in all directions. As well as the trig point at 757 feet (230 metres) there is a concrete plinth, no doubt once bearing a steel or brass

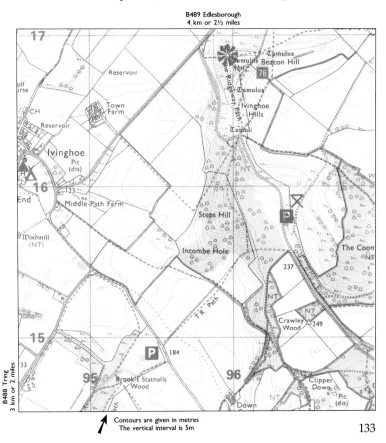

B489 Edlesborough
4 km or 2½ miles

Contours are given in metres
The vertical interval is 5m

The chalk grassland slopes of Ivinghoe Beacon, which signify the end – or start – of the Ridgeway.

plaque indicating everything that can be seen to all points of the compass but long since stolen.

The walk is done and it is now just a matter of finding one's way home. The easiest way to the village of Ivinghoe is along the B489, which does have a pavement for walkers. Ivinghoe has a smart restaurant for anyone who wishes to celebrate their endeavours in style, and there is a youth hostel in the Old Brewery House with a pub a little further up the road towards Pitstone. You might like to visit the 13th century church of St Mary the Virgin, which has a thatch hook once used to pull burning thatch from houses to prevent fire from spreading and, beneath it, there is a man trap.

If you feel like walking further, Ivinghoe Beacon is not just the end (or beginning) of the Ridgeway; it is also the start of the Two Ridges Link to the Greensand Ridge Walk, and the Icknield Way if you fancy going on to Norfolk. But perhaps that is for another day, and another journey.

PART THREE

USEFUL
INFORMATION

Transport

To help you plan your outings along the Ridgeway, a checklist of towns and villages served by public transport follows (listed from west to east). Full details of local bus operators are included in the *Ridgeway Accommodation Guide* (see page 141).

Avebury: buses to Marlborough, Devizes and Swindon (BR station)

Pewsey: BR station – then walk to Overton Hill

Ogbourne St George: frequent Swindon–Marlborough buses, weekdays only

Wanborough: buses to Swindon, Marlborough and Newbury (infrequent)

Bishopstone: buses to Swindon

Ashbury: buses to Swindon

Woolstone: buses to Wantage

Uffington: buses to Wantage and Faringdon, but infrequent service

Sparsholt: infrequent buses to Wantage

Letcombe Regis/Childrey: infrequent buses to Wantage

Wantage: buses to Oxford and Didcot (BR stations) and London, as well as to local villages

Lockinge and Ardington: buses to Wantage, Didcot, Oxford

Chilton: buses to Oxford and Newbury (BR station)

West Ilsley: infrequent bus to Newbury

East Ilsley: buses to Oxford, Newbury, Southampton

Compton: buses to Newbury

Blewbury: infrequent buses to Didcot

Goring/Streatley: BR station – trains to Oxford, Reading and London and buses to Wallingford and Reading (no Sunday buses anywhere)

Wallingford: buses to Oxford, Reading (no Sunday service), Didcot (no Sunday service) and London

Nuffield Common: buses to Wallingford, Henley-on-Thames (BR station), Oxford and London

Watlington: buses to Oxford, Reading and Henley-on-Thames

Lewknor: buses to Thame, Watlington, Oxford and London

Aston Rowant: buses to Oxford, High Wycombe (BR station) and London

Chinnor: buses to High Wycombe and Thame
Princes Risborough: BR station: London–Aylesbury line and buses to Aylesbury, High Wycombe, London, Birmingham, Milton Keynes, Northampton, Banbury and Warwick
Great Kimble: buses to High Wycombe and Aylesbury
Little Kimble: BR station
Wendover: BR station: London–Aylesbury line, plus buses to Aylesbury
Wigginton: buses to Chesham and Tring
Tring: BR station: London–Milton Keynes line, plus buses to Aylesbury and Watford
Ivinghoe: buses to Cheddington, Luton and Aylesbury (all BR stations)

Rail
From London
Paddington Station, tel. (01) 262 6767 – Intercity to Swindon, Didcot, Reading, Newbury, Oxford, Pewsey. Local service to Goring on Thames.
Marylebone Station, tel. (01) 387 7070 – local services to Saunderton, Princes Risborough, Wendover.
Euston Station, tel. (01) 387 7070 – local service to Tring and Cheddington.
St Pancras Station, tel. (01) 278 2477 – local service to Luton.

From the West Country and South Wales
Intercity to Swindon, Didcot, Reading, Newbury, Pewsey.

From the Midlands and the North
Intercity to Oxford, Didcot, Reading, Luton, Milton Keynes.

From the South Coast
Intercity to Reading and Luton.

Accommodation

The *Ridgeway Accommodation Guide* (see page 141) includes addresses of bed and breakfast/guesthouse accommodation and details of camp sites, hostels, etc. To help you plan your journey here is a checklist of places where accommodation is available.

Marlborough: hotels, b & b
Avebury: b & b
Winterbourne Monkton (near Avebury): b & b
Ogbourne St George: b & b, guesthouse

Aldbourne: pub

Fox Hill: camping at pub, Shepherd's Rest, tel. Swindon (0793) 790266

Ashbury: pub

Uffington: b & b, guesthouse

Letcombe Regis: b & b

Wantage: Court Hill Ridgeway Centre, Court Hill, Letcombe Regis, tel. Wantage (02357) 60253 (see page 64) – self-catering hostel-type accommodation plus camping. Wantage itself has hotels, guest houses and b & b accommodation.

East Hendred: b & b

East Ilsley: pub

Streatley: youth hostel, Hill House, tel. Goring on Thames (0491) 872278

Goring on Thames: pubs, b & b

Wallingford: pubs, guesthouses, b & b, plus South Oxfordshire District Council camp site by river (tel. Wallingford (0491) 35351)

Benson: pubs, b & b

Watlington: hotel plus camp site at White Mark Farm, 82 Hill Road, tel. Watlington (049161) 2295

Lewknor: b & b

Aston Rowant: guesthouse

Bledlow: b & b

Princes Risborough: pubs, guesthouses, b & b

Great Kimble: pub

Wendover: hotels, b & b

Tring: hotels, b & b

Ivinghoe: youth hostel and camping – The Old Brewery House, tel. Aylesbury (0296) 668251

Stabling for horses

In many cases, the following places can offer accommodation for riders as well.

Ogbourne St George: Foxlynch Junior Training Centre, Foxlynch, Ogbourne St George, tel. Ogbourne St George (067284) 307

Aldbourne: The Crown at Aldbourne, The Square, Aldbourne, tel. Marlborough (0672) 40214

East Hendred: Ridgeway Lodge, Skeets Bush, Newbury Road, East Hendred, Wantage, tel. Didcot (0235) 833360

Wantage: Court Hill Ridgeway Centre, Court Hill, Letcombe Regis, tel. Wantage (02357) 60253; White Horse Stables, Brook Cottage, Charney Bassett, Wantage, tel. Wantage (023587) 492

Harwell: Silverdown Riding School, Reading Road, Harwell, Didcot, tel. Didcot (0235) 835377

Benson: Hale Farm, Benson, tel. Wallingford (0491) 36818

Lewknor: The Manor House, Lewknor, tel. Kingston Blount (0844) 51680

Bledlow: The Gables, Skittle Green, Bledlow, tel. Princes Risborough (08444) 4392

Askett: The Bell House Barn, Crowbrook Road, Askett, Aylesbury, tel. Princes Risborough (08444) 6107

The British Horse Society publishes *Bed and Breakfast for Horses: Stabling and Grazing*. Details from BHS, Bridleways Dept, British Equestrian Centre, Stoneleigh, Kenilworth, Warks, CV8 2LR.

Tourist information centres

These are useful for advice about local services and can usually book accommodation in advance.

Seasonal centres at:

Marlborough: St Peter's Church, High Street, Marlborough, Wilts, SN8 1HQ, tel. Marlborough (0672) 53989

Avebury: The Great Barn, Avebury, Nr Marlborough, Wilts, SN8 1RF, tel. Avebury (06723) 425

Centres open all year at:

Wallingford: 9 St Martin's Street, Wallingford, Oxon, OX10 0AL, tel. Wallingford (0491) 35351 ex. 3810

Wendover: Clock Tower, High Street, Wendover, Bucks, HP22 6DU, tel. Wendover (0296) 623056

For regional information, contact either of the tourist boards in the area:

Thames and Chilterns Tourist Board, Mount House, Witney, Oxon, OX8 6DZ, tel. Witney (0993) 778800.

West Country Tourist Board, 37 Southernhay East, Exeter, EX1 1QS, tel. Exeter (0392) 76351.

Another useful source of information about accommodation is the Ramblers' Association *Yearbook*. Published annually, it is available free to members. Contact the Ramblers' Association, 1/5 Wandsworth Road, London, SW8 2XX.

Town and village facilities

Public houses are marked on the maps, but the following list may be useful for those who are not familiar with the area:

Marlborough: all town services
Avebury: shops, café, National Trust shop, museum, toilets
Ogbourne St George: shops, café, garage
Aldbourne: shops, fish and chips, bank, garage, toilets, launderette
Bishopstone: store, post office, restaurant
Ashbury: shop, post office
Lambourn: most services
Uffington: shops, post office, village hall teas on Sundays, museum, police station
Childrey and Letcombe Regis: shops, post office, garage (sells camping and Calor gas)
Wantage: all town services
Lockinge and Ardington: shops, post office
East Hendred: shop, post office
Chilton: shop, post office
West Ilsley: shop, post office, vet
East Ilsley: shop, post office, saddler
Compton: shops, post office, garage, doctor's surgery, bank (limited hours)
Blewbury: shop, post office, garage
Streatley: grocers/cheese shop
Goring on Thames: shops, banks, post office
South Stoke: shop
North Stoke: refreshments in church hall, summer Sundays and bank holidays
Wallingford: all town services (including a butcher selling additive-free meat, wholefood shop and a wine vault)
Watlington: a variety of services, including fish and chips
Lewknor: shop/post office
Kingston Blount: shop, post office
Chinnor: most services
Princes Risborough: most services
Wendover: most services
Wigginton: shop (open on Sundays as well)
Tring: all town services, plus zoological museum
Pitstone: café
Ivinghoe: shops, bank (Thursday only), restaurant

Responsibility for the Ridgeway

The Ridgeway has been designated as a national trail by the Countryside Commission, which funds the post of Ridgeway Officer and most of the maintenance costs. The five county councils through which the Ridgeway runs – Wiltshire, Oxfordshire, Berkshire, Buckinghamshire and Hertfordshire – are responsible for managing the route and for maintenance work, waymarking, etc.

The Ridgeway Officer, based with Oxfordshire County Council, coordinates the management of the Ridgeway, including surface maintenance, and liaises with landowners where there may be problems. A team of wardens assists the Ridgeway Officer on summer Sundays and bank holidays (and at times in the winter). There is also an active programme of 'Discovery Walks'.

A *Ridgeway Information Pack* is available which includes the *Accommodation Guide*, 'Discovery Walks' programmes and circular walks leaflets. Requests for the pack and all queries about the Ridgeway should be addressed to: Ridgeway Officer, Countryside Section, Library Headquarters, Holton, Oxford, OX9 1QQ, tel. Oxford (0865) 810224.

A voluntary society, Friends of the Ridgeway, also takes an interest in the national trail. New members are welcomed; enquiries should be directed to: The Secretary, Friends of the Ridgeway, 90 South Hill Park, London, NW3 2SN.

Regional recreational routes

A number of regional routes for walking and riding connect with the Ridgeway and therefore provide the opportunity for further extensive journeys on foot or on horseback.

The Wessex Ridgeway: a 137-mile (220-km) walk from Lyme Regis in Dorset to Marlborough. A route devised by the Ramblers' Association, which has published a guide (1988) price £2.50 (plus 40p p&p) obtainable from their London office.

The Thames Path: although the proposed national trail along the Thames will not be complete for a number of years, it is possible to walk much of the riverside route. Two guidebooks are available: *Thames Walk* (Ramblers' Association, 1981) and *The Thames Path* (Constable, 1988). Further information on the progress of the Thames Path can be obtained from the Countryside Commission's South East Office (see page 142).

Swan's Way: a new 65-mile (104-km) bridleway from Goring

on Thames to Salcey Forest, Northants. Contact Buckinghamshire County Council, County Engineers Dept, County Hall, Aylesbury, Bucks, HP20 1UA (SAE please) for details.

Oxfordshire Way: a 65-mile (104-km) walk from Henley-on-Thames to Bourton on the Water in the Cotswolds. Information available from Oxfordshire County Council, Leisure and Arts Department, Central Library, Westgate, Oxford, OX1 1DJ.

North Bucks Way: this 30-mile (48-km) route from Chequers Knap to Wolverton has recently been reopened. Information is available from the Ramblers' Association (see page 139) or from Bucks County Council (see above).

Icknield Way: connects with the Peddars Way in Norfolk, thus making it possible to walk from Lyme Regis in Dorset to the North Norfolk coast. Details from the Icknield Way Association, 19 Boundary Road, Bishop's Stortford, Herts, CM23 5LE.

Greensand Ridge Walk: a 30-mile (48-km) walk from Leighton Buzzard to Tetworth in Cambridge. Linked to the Ridgeway by the Two Ridges Link. Information about the former from Bedfordshire County Council, Dept of Leisure Services, Bedford, MK42 9AP, and on the latter from Bucks County Council.

Other useful addresses

All Wheel Drive Club, PO Box 6, Fleet, Hampshire, GU13 9YY

Backpacker's Club, 20 St Michael's Road, Tilehurst, Reading, RG3 4RP

Berkshire, Buckinghamshire and Oxfordshire Naturalists Trust (BBONT), 3 Church Cowley Road, Cowley, Oxford

Byways and Bridleways Trust, 9 Queen Anne's Gate, London, SW1H 9BH

Chiltern Society, Assistant Gen. Secretary, 60 The Row, Lane End, High Wycombe, Bucks, HP14 3JU

Countryside Commission (Headquarters), John Dower House, Crescent Place, Cheltenham, Glos, GL50 3RA

Countryside Commission (South East Regional Office), 71 Kingsway, London, WC2B 6ST

Cyclists Touring Club, 69 Meadrow, Godalming, Surrey, GU7 3HS

Endurance Horse and Pony Society of Great Britain, 15 Newport Drive, Alcester, Warks, B49 5BL

Land Access and Rights Association, Mill House, Corporation Street, Rugby, Warks, CV21 2DN

Long Distance Walkers Association, 29 Appledown Road, Alresford, Hampshire, SO24 9ND

National Off-road Bicycle Association, 139 Tooley Street, London, SE1 2NZ

National Trust (Thames and Chilterns Regional Information), Hughenden Manor, High Wycombe, Bucks, HP14 4LA

Ordnance Survey, Romsey Road, Maybush, Southampton, S09 4DH. Tel. Southampton (0703) 792792.

Oxford Fieldpaths Society, 21 Rowles Close, Kennington, Oxford, OX1 5LZ

Trail Riders Fellowship, 11 Askew Drive, Spencers Wood, Reading, Berks, RG7 1HG

Wiltshire Trust for Nature Conservation, 19 High Street, Devizes, Wilts

Youth Hostels Association, Trevelyan House, 8 St Stephen Hill, St Albans, Herts, AL1 2DY

Bibliography

Bulfield, Anthony, *The Icknield Way* (Terence Dalton, 1972).

Burden, Vera *et al*, *Discovering the Ridgeway* (Shire Publications, 1985).

Charles, Alan, *Exploring the Ridgeway* (Countryside Books, 1988).

Fitter, R. (ed.), *The Wildlife of the Thames Counties* (BBONT/ Robert Dugdale, 1985).

Godwin, Fay and Anderson, J. R. L., *The Oldest Road: An Exploration of the Ridgeway* (Whittet Books, 1987).

Ingrams, Richard, *The Ridgeway* (Phaidon Press, 1988).

Ordnance Survey Historical Guides, *Oxfordshire and Berkshire* (OS and George Philip, 1988).

Pitts, Michael, *Footprints through Avebury* (Stones Print, 1985).

Stewart, Pamela, *The Bridleways of Britain* (Whittet Books, 1986): includes a route for horseriders from Goring to Ivinghoe.

Thomas, Edward, *The Icknield Way* (Wildwood, 1980).

de M. Vatcher, Faith and Vatcher, Lance, *The Avebury Monuments* (English Heritage, 1987).

Ordnance Survey Maps covering the Ridgeway

Landranger Maps: 165, 173, 174, 175.

Pathfinder Maps: 1094(SP81/91), 1117 (SP60/70)
1118(SP80/90), 1137(SU69/79)
1154(SU28/38), 1155(SU48/58)
1156(SU68/78),1169(SU07/17)
1170(SU27/37), 1185(SU06/16)

Motoring Maps: Reach the Ridgeway area using Routemaster Map 9, 'South East England'.

A note to the National Trail Guide user

We hope you like your National Trail Guide.

A great deal of care has been given to accuracy and clarity in compiling these guides but, inevitably, improvements can be made.

To help the publishers in making these books as accurate and useful as possible, your comments and criticisms are welcomed. Please write, giving your own name, address and postcode, and stating which guide(s) you have bought, to the following Freepost address (no stamp required): Countryside Commission, Freepost (GR 1422), Cheltenham, Glos, GL50 3BR.

In return we are offering a new service to you, the user. You will receive a newsletter containing additional information and revisions to help you make the most of the guides and enjoy your walks to the full.